Long ago, before the world began, Satan and some of the angels rebelled against God and there was war in heaven. God saw that Satan must be defeated by creatures no higher in the scale of being – and so he embarked on the Creation. So our purpose is to wage war on Satan and bring him to repentance.

In this provocative book, Norman Dockeray shows us where Satan is winning and how we can change our lives to resist his wiles and fulfil God's purpose for us. He also tells us which are the inventions – or perversions – of Satan. For now, 2000 years after Christ, the battle is being fought with new weapons. But the kingdom of heaven is at hand, ready to be grasped . . .

Norman Dockeray was born near Dublin in 1902, was educated in Dublin, Belfast and at Emmanuel College, Cambridge, where he obtained a First Class degree in Mathematics. After teaching for many years at Dulwich College and Harrow School, he joined the Ministry of Food at the beginning of the Second World War and remained a civil servant until 1961. He was awarded a CBE in 1962. Mr Dockeray worked for a further eight years as secretary to the Covent Garden Market Authority.

His early works were on mathematics and mechanics but since his retirement he has concentrated on theology and has written 'An Anglican's reflections on *Humanae Vitae*' which was published in the Catholic 'Downside Review', articles on 'The Fatherhood of God', 'Thy kingdom come – on Earth', and two previous books both published by The Book Guild: *Tentative Answers to Ten Questions* in 1988 and *The Power of Miracle* in 1991.

Theological Publications by Norman Dockeray:

An Anglican's Reflections on Humanae Vitae, Downside Review, July 1970

The Fatherhood of God, The Dulwich Villager, 1971

Tentative Answers to Ten Questions, The Book Guild, 1988

Thy Kingdom Come, on Earth, Fairacres Chronicle, Spring 1989

The Power of Miracle, The Book Guild, 1991

THE REDEMPTION OF SATAN

Norman R C Dockeray, CBE

The Book Guild Ltd
Sussex, England

This book is sold subject to the condition that it shall not, by way of trade or otherwise, be lent, re-sold, hired out, photocopied or held in any retrieval system or otherwise circulated without the publisher's prior consent in any form of binding or cover other than that in which this is published and without a similar condition including this condition being imposed on the subsequent purchaser.

The Book Guild Ltd,
25 High Street,
Lewes, Sussex

First published 1999
© Norman Dockeray 1999

Set in Times
Typesetting by
Acorn Bookwork, Salisbury, Wiltshire

Printed in Great Britain by
Athenaeum Press Ltd, Gateshead

A catalogue record for this book is
available from the British Library

ISBN 1 85776 349 1

To Barbara

CONTENTS

Foreword		ix
Preface		xi
1	The Insufficiency of Personal Salvation	1
2	The New Strategy	21
3	The Conduct of the War and the Conquest of Death	57
	Summary	57
	Weapons and Armoury	66
	Satan's Tactics	74
	God's Interventions	91
4	Implications, Inferences and Initial Steps	106
	The Kingdom of God	106
	An Analogy	109
	Evil and Sin	113
	Suffering	120
	The Moral Code	122
	Economics	125
	Science and Technology	129
	Restraints	136
5	The End and the Beginning	146
Index		161

FOREWORD

The postmodern mind lives not only with perpetual ambiguity, it doubts whether there is any other stance to take on fundamental issues. It looks out on a world which it regards as perplexing and ultimately unknowable, where history offers us few clues for all tradition has to be deconstructed. The problem is that most people cannot live within postmodernity for very long. There is something in the human heart which longs for explanation, and for a reality which has abiding value and truth.

Into this context comes Norman Dockeray's latest book. His refusal to be satisfied with the ambiguity of our age cuts into so many of the debates which are current. It is regrettable that his earlier books, *Tentative Answers to Ten Questions* and *The Power of Miracle* are now out of print, for they illustrate this refusal well. He does not duck the difficulties of addressing diversity of opinion, especially when that diversity is to be found amongst those who have made these areas of enquiry their own. But his assurance is that either the necessity of finding an answer will disappear with the passage of time, or that God will reveal the answer when we are sufficiently mature to understand it.

The originality and relevance of his ideas for today which are also evidenced in these earlier books can be found displayed in *The Redemption of Satan*. The theme is an ambitious one. It is an inquiry into why God created the human race and also a universe of such enormous magnitude, complexity and splendour that those who stop to contemplate the reality of such a universe are inevitably filled with awe. This is true of people even in postmodern society. For if God created the human heart, that heart may be ultimately opened to the truth about reality, whatever the cultural context.

Dockeray assumes that the actions and plans of God are at the heart of reality, which is therefore purposeful. This purpose underlies everything that God does and everything he refrains from doing, and human beings themselves are drawn in. For all beings endowed with freedom, wherever they exist in the universe, may be involved in playing a significant part in the purposes of God. But sin has always to be taken into consideration. For sin makes us not only cruel and self-centred, it also makes us gullible. Satan, the father of lies, has been effective in his work with human beings. He attempts to persuade us both that he does not exist and that what is evil is in fact good. Yet Satan will not have the final victory. Dockeray argues, carefully and convincingly, that the Incarnation, Crucifixion and Resurrection of Christ are the powerful acts of the God who is love. They are the inevitable events in the working out of God's purpose.

The activities of Satan are not minimised in this book. Dockeray does not spare us when he examines the evil consequences which flow from them. He never minimises the difficulties which Satan leaves in the paths of even the wise and godly. He offers certain practical steps in resisting and frustrating his evil designs. But Dockeray's chief contribution is his confidence (as in his previous books) that Satan will ultimately be defeated and that the kingdom of God will be established on earth.

I was delighted to be asked to write this foreword to what I know will be a well-received book. My students have already been exposed to Norman Dockeray's work, and there has been no shortage of discussion and debate. I shall encourage them to tackle this latest book for those who come to his work with inquiring minds find there is much there to stimulate the brain cells. Dockeray does not expect that all will agree with him. But he certainly has every reason to believe that readers will find his contribution valuable and full of insight. I do hope his work reaches well into the twenty-first century, and even outlives the author himself. For it will stand as a fitting legacy to a tenacious thinker in theology and religious study.

Dr Elaine Storkey
Director, Institute for Contemporary Christianity 1991-98
London 1998

PREFACE

Today, because of the rapid pace of change, we are impelled, more forcibly than ever before in human history, to ask Why are we here? Where are we going? What is the ultimate destiny of the human race, both in time and in eternity? To these questions I give a partial answer in this book. This is an ambitious programme, and the answers given must necessarily be incomplete, for much remains to be revealed, but it is a task that cannot be shirked. For in everything that God has done he has had a purpose and it is our duty to discover that purpose and to work towards its fulfilment. He had a purpose in creating the angels, in creating the universe of space, time and matter, and in devising the immensely intricate laws of nature. He had a purpose in creating life and mind, and in investing them with an evolutionary impetus directed to the fulfilment of that purpose, giving rise to the wonderful variety of living creatures that have inhabited the earth in the past, that inhabit it today, and that will inhabit it in centuries yet unborn. All these creations must therefore be honoured. Above all, he had a purpose in creating men and women in his image, in giving them a spiritual dimension whereby they can respond to his love and can, at least in part, comprehend and serve his purpose, and in endowing them with free will and with intelligence whereby they are enabled to understand the nature and the laws of the universe in which he has placed them.

In all these acts of creation there lies a mystery and it is our duty to strive to find the meaning hidden in this mystery. We have been partially enlightened by scripture and other sacred writings, and what we learn from these has been supplemented by the work of philosophers and theologians, of scientists, of artists, musicians and poets, and of inspired writers of fiction.

We are all under a duty to use the faculties with which we are endowed and to discharge the earthly tasks in which we are engaged in such a way as to increase our understanding of God's purpose, for we are his chosen agents in the unfolding and achievement of that purpose. And this is true however humble our task may be in the eyes of the world.

Obviously, in attempting to answer the questions posed above one must make assumptions on which to build, but in order to avoid clogging the investigation or misdirecting it by falsehoods, these should be kept to a minimum. In the argument set out in the following pages I have made only three basic assumptions – that God exists, that he has a will and that he is rational. From the fact that he has a will we deduce that he is active, for an idle will is a contradiction in terms; and from the fact that he is rational we deduce that his activity is not capricious but is directed to a purpose.

Acceptance of these assumptions is of course a matter of faith. But denial of them is equally a matter of faith, and is tenable only if certain characteristics of human nature are ignored. These include the fact that human beings can grasp the concept of truth and have a reverence for it, that they have an appreciation of beauty that goes far beyond what is necessary to attract a mate and to ensure the survival of the species, and that they have a concept of duty and a moral sense that cannot be attributed solely to an evolutionary development of enlightened self-interest.

The book is written from a Christian point of view, and I have therefore also accepted the truth that God was incarnate in Jesus Christ. But I have argued, I hope successfully, that this is not really an additional assumption; that in fact the possibility of the Incarnation was inherent in God from before the beginning of time, and that he knew that for the achievement of his purpose it would almost certainly become inevitable, because all created beings are necessarily less, in all essential particulars, than their Creator.

In the search to discover God's purpose and in the effort to bring it to fruition, the development of 'pentecostal' practices, which have been so marked a feature of the present century, have a contribution to make, but the practices they espouse must be treated with caution. In many cases they are simply expressions, not of the activity of the Holy Spirit, but of physical and mental emotion, which are freed from all inhibitions and are allowed to dominate the soul. The kingdom of God cannot be built, nor can the salvation of humankind be achieved, by this reversal of the true order of priority. What is needed at the present time is a recovery of the rigidity of logical argument which was characteristic of the theology of the Middle Ages, and my object in the present book has been to direct the development of theological speculation along this path.

1

The Insufficiency of Personal Salvation

The central event in the history of the human race is the Incarnation of God in Jesus Christ, an event which was inevitably followed by the Crucifixion of Jesus and his resurrection and ascension. The recognition and the belief that these events were always, from the beginning, a possibility, and that they did in fact occur, together with all the implications of that belief, are what distinguishes Christianity from all other theistic religions – they are its defining characteristics.

But they do not constitute its foundations. This is obvious, for in the statement of those characteristic events we refer to God; it therefore involves the assumption that God exists, and the question whether this assumption is valid is the most fundamental question that can possibly be asked. It leads at once to other fundamental questions: if God exists, is he a lifeless Absolute or a living Being, and if he is a living Being what is his nature?

Christianity asserts unequivocally that God is a living Being and that he has a will embodying a purpose. This follows from the fact that at a certain point in time he did something very remarkable, that he acted in a very specific way. It would indeed be absurd to suppose that God has ever acted capriciously. We cannot liken his actions to those of a child wandering along the seashore, picking up a pebble or a shell, looking at it and then throwing it away, and repeating the action from time to time. In allowing from the beginning, before time and space existed, for the possibility of the Incarnation, God must have had a purpose, and since the Incarnation affects every member of the human race personally, and the human race as a whole, it is obvious that we are involved in that purpose; we must therefore seek to discover what it is and what part we have to play in its fulfilment.

The simplest answer to these two questions is the one we are given in childhood. In the words of the Presbyterian catechism, we have been created to glorify God and to enjoy him for ever. To show us how to do this God has laid down certain rules, which are embodied in the commandment to love him with all our heart, with all our soul and with all our might (Deuteronomy vi, 5), and to serve him (Deuteronomy x, 12), to keep his commandments (Deuteronomy x, 13), and to love our neighbour as ourself (Leviticus xix, 18). More specifically, we are given the Ten Commandments (Exodus xx, 1–17). We must not worship false gods; we must honour those to whom God has given authority; we must not murder or commit adultery: we must not steal or even covet our neighbour's goods. Moreover, we must make provision for the poor, for widows and orphans, and strangers in our land, whom we must treat as our kin (Leviticus xix, 10; Deuteronomy xiv, 29; xxiv, 19–21; xxvi, 12). Christ has extended the literal meaning of these commandments by telling us that merely to harbour the thought of disobeying them is an infringement of God's laws (Matthew v, 21, 22, 27, 28). He has also added to them by laying down rules of behaviour; tending the sick, clothing the naked, visiting prisoners, feeding the hungry, as described by Matthew in the twenty-fifth chapter of his gospel. We have obviously failed to fulfil these requirements, in varying degrees, and by our failure we have alienated ourselves from God and have incurred a penalty. But by his death on the Cross Christ has redeemed us and has atoned for our sins; he has paid the penalty and has reconciled us to his Father, who is God. Also by his resurrection and ascension he has assured us of the possibility of eternal life, a possibility that becomes a certainty if we repent of our sins. But at the end of time, on the last day (John vi, 40), he will return to judge 'the quick and the dead' (2 Timothy iv, 1; 1 Peter iv, 5) and to award the gift of eternal life to those who are found worthy.

This account of the major points of current Christian belief is of course incomplete; it omits the doctrinal points contained in the creeds and in the decisions made by the early councils of the church. Briefly, the creeds tell us that God is the creator of everything that has being, including those things that have temporal (i.e. physical or mental) being and those that have eternal (or spiritual) being. They also tell us that God is three Persons, that it was in the Person of the Son that he took on human flesh and that his earthly mother was the Virgin Mary. The Father and the Son are 'of the same substance', and the third Person of the Trinity is the Holy Spirit, by whom Mary became pregnant, and who proceeds from the Father and the Son. The Holy Spirit is also the Paraclete, which means counsellor or advocate, in this capacity he pleads the cause of God to us human beings, who would otherwise be tempted to reject him*. From the early councils we learn that Christ had (and still has) two 'natures', human and divine, and that he also had two wills, human and divine, his human will being in all respects subject to and in accord with his divine will.

We need not, however, concern ourselves with these doctrinal points, which remain valid whatever answer we give to the two questions posed on page 1. We therefore return to a consideration of the 'simple' answer given on page 2, which may be taken, either as it stands or as modified by the Roman Catholic doctrine of Purgatory, as being the answer accepted by the majority of Christians today. According to this answer we have to believe that during our life on earth (and in Purgatory) we are undergoing a test which we either pass or fail. If we pass the test we shall be rewarded and if we fail we will be punished.

In this interpretation of what Christianity demands, the emphasis is on personal salvation. We are charged with the responsibility of conducting our lives in such a manner as to earn the reward of admission to heaven, where we shall live eternally with Christ as our friend. Whether we succeed or fail depends entirely on how we conduct ourselves during our

---

*The Holy Spirit does not advocate our cause with God the Father; this task is reserved to the Son (1 John ii, 1).

earthly life. (If we believe in Purgatory, it should be added that failure can be changed to success if our experiences there bring about repentance for our sins on earth.) The criterion is an individual, not a communal, issue; each one of us has to pass the test personally. It is of course true that to pass the test we must have regard to the well-being of our neighbours, even to love them, but this is a personal, not a communal, requirement, although in practice it may involve communal action. It is also true that we pray that God's kingdom may be established on earth, and we believe that when this has been done the lives of all people on earth will be transformed, but we do not think of this as a communal task, dedicated to communal salvation; we tend to think that, provided that we seek our own personal salvation by obeying God's commandments, the task of building his kingdom on earth may be left to him; all we have to do, individually, is to pray 'Thy kingdom come, thy will be done, on earth' with true sincerity; the fulfilment of this prayer can, indeed must, be left to God.

When, however, we come to examine this interpretation (which we may call 'the test theory'*) in detail, we find that it is very unsatisfactory. It is, of course, not wholly wrong, but it is certainly incomplete. The first difficulty we encounter is that, although on the surface the Ten Commandments appear to be clear and specific, we find when we try to apply them to particular circumstances that they leave us without adequate guidance. We are told we must not murder, but most people would say that if we kill a man in self-defence we have done no wrong. Christ, on the other hand, when he was arrested, knowing that he would be condemned to death, said that he could call upon twelve legions of angels to save him (Matthew xxvi, 53), but he refrained from doing so. He also told us that if anyone strikes us on the right cheek we should turn to him the other also (Matthew v, 39), and this instruction may also extend to any attack, however severe. But we do not know whether, in order to pass the test, we are called on to make

---

*'My son, if you aspire to be a servant of the Lord, prepare yourself for testing' (Ecclesiasticus ii, 1).

this extension. Is it right or wrong for a soldier to kill enemy soldiers in a 'just' war, and indeed can it ever be said that a war is just? Is it right or wrong in such a war to kill enemy civilians, bearing in mind that civilians bear a responsibility, which is at least as great as that of any soldier, for bringing about the circumstances which made war inevitable? This problem is rendered all the more difficult by the fact that, if the scriptures are true, God himself broke his own commandment on many occasions, as for example when he instructed Samuel to tell Saul to attack the Amalekites and totally destroy them and all their possessions. Saul was ordered to spare none; God required him to slaughter men and women, children and infants, cattle and sheep, camels and donkeys (1 Samuel xv, 3). If any dictator today were to treat an enemy in such a manner we should regard him as a monster. Later, when Samuel discovered that Saul had not carried out these instructions fully, but had spared the Amalekite king Agag and also the best of the cattle and sheep, he told Saul that he would be punished for his disobedience* (1 Samuel xv, 12–33); and this judgment was confirmed by the witch of Endor (1 Samuel xxviii, 3–19).

The commandment 'Love your neighbour as yourself' is amplified in the teaching of Christ, who exhorted us to love not only our neighbours but also our enemies, to do good to those who hate us, and to pray for those who persecute us (Matthew v, 44). He also extolled the virtues of meekness (humility), mercy, purity, hungering for righteousness, peacemaking and the patient endurance of persecution (Matthew v, 3–10). And he emphasised that evil thoughts are sinful and can damage the soul even if they are not carried into action (Matthew v, 21, 22, 27, 28). These exhortations, indeed the whole of the sermon on the mount (Matthew v–vii) are nourishing food for the soul, and we should constantly strive

---

*The only plausible explanation of these events is that Samuel was misled; it was not God who instructed him but Satan, whose ability to masquerade as God is almost unlimited, and is being put to evil use today with as much vigour and with equally devastating consequences as in the time of Saul.

so to order our evolution as to make them directly applicable to our daily lives, but we find it difficult to see how they can be applied to the moral problems that we encounter in the present state of the world. The merciful do not always receive mercy, nor do we expect the meek to inherit the earth. The reason for this incompatibility is, of course, not that the precepts of the sermon are wrong, but that the pattern of life we have built up is widely divergent from that which God has designed for us at this stage of our evolution; it is therefore to the task of remodelling our present pattern of life that we must direct our attention.

This, however, will be a task requiring many hundreds of years, and our immediate problem is to discover how we can best interpret the Commandments and the teaching of Christ in relation to our present circumstances. This is not easy, and many instances of the difficulty of interpretation could be cited. Is abortion murder, and if so is it ever justified? Should those who break God's laws or the laws made by human beings be treated as criminals and punished or as invalids in need of psychiatric treatment? Or does the answer to this question depend on circumstances? Is it right or wrong to conduct experiments in genetic engineering and, in particular, to transfer human genes to animals? We know, or at least most people believe, that human beings, uniquely, possess souls as well as minds and bodies, but we do not know whether a 'portion' of soul resides in every human cell, in the nucleus of every cell and in every gene. If this is the case then by transplanting human genes we are interfering in a fundamental way with God's design, in which a clear distinction between human beings, who are made 'in his image', and other animals is made. Is this right or wrong? Is it right or wrong to use animals in experiments which, it is claimed, may lead to a cure for or the prevention of some human ailment? More generally, should scientists be given a free hand to conduct experiments which may (or may not) lead to a fuller understanding of God's universe, or should they be restricted by some moral imperative and, if so, what is that imperative?

On a larger scale, are we right or wrong in trying to impose

Western culture, Western economics and Western political systems on those to whom all these are alien and who, not because they are wicked but because they are different, either reject or misapply them? We do not know the answers to these questions. Nor do we know whether the moral issues involved in them are absolute and unalterable or are contingent and dependent on the prevailing circumstances. And in the latter case, what circumstances should be taken into account?

It may be said that in asking these questions we are merely quibbling. Many people would argue that in addition to Christ's teaching we have his life to guide us. We have only to model our lives on his life and all will be well. This argument may sound persuasive, but it is unhelpful, for in fact we know very little about the life of Jesus. The gospels tell us about the miracles he performed, but they tell us practically nothing about how he coped with the ordinary problems of life. How did he earn his living? We are told that Joseph, who was generally supposed to be his father, was a carpenter (Matthew xii, 55), and Mark, recording the same fact, says that Jesus followed the same trade (Mark vi, 3). But he seems to have spent very little time in Nazareth. He was a rabbi, entitled to preach in the synagogue and in the Temple in Jerusalem, and after his thirtieth year (Luke iii, 23) he spent the greater part of his time in moving from place to place, healing the sick and teaching the crowds who flocked to hear him wherever he went. He was baptised by John in Bethabara in the south of Galilee (Mark i, 9–11; John i, 28–34), and he visited Cana, Capernaum, Nain and other places in Galilee. He crossed the Jordan to Bethsaida, just north of the Sea of Galilee, where he fed the five thousand (Luke ix, 10–17) and where he healed a blind man (Mark viii, 22–26), and to Caesarea Philippi, where Peter acknowledged him to be the Son of God (Matthew xvi, 13–20). He also went to Phoenicia 'to the border of Tyre and Sidon' (Mark vii, 24) and possibly also to the region of the Decapolis, where he was certainly well known (Matthew iv, 25).

When he was in Judaea he visited Bethany (Mark xiv, 3), Jericho (Luke xix, 1) and Ephraim (John xi, 54), and he paid several visits to Jerusalem before the final visit which led to his crucifixion. This, of course, is recorded by all four evangelists (Matthew xxi, 1–16; Mark xi, 1–11; Luke xix, 28–48; John xii, 12–19). John records three earlier visits: on the first of these he drove the moneylenders out of the Temple (John ii, 13–17); on the second he went there for the Feast of the Tabernacles (John vii, 2–15), when we are told that the Jews, believing him to be uneducated, marvelled at his teaching (verse 15). The third visit was for the Feast of Dedication, when the Jews asked him to state plainly whether he was the Messiah, and at the end of this discourse in reply he said 'I and my Father are one' (John x, 22–30). The synoptic evangelists also record visits to Jerusalem (see, for example, Luke ix, 51–53); these may, or may not, have coincided with those recorded by John.

Jesus was of course unmarried and had no dependants, and this gave him a measure of freedom to travel. But he seems to have had no difficulty in the course of his travels in finding food and shelter for himself and those of his disciples who were constantly with him. He claimed to have no home – 'The foxes have holes, and the birds of the air have nests, but the Son of man hath not where to lay his head' (Matthew viii, 20) – and it is probable that when he was teaching within walking or riding distance of Nazareth he lived with his mother Mary and Joseph. It would seem that during his wanderings further afield he relied on the native hospitality of the Jews, epitomised in Abraham's welcoming three strangers (Genesis xviii, 1–8) and Lot's inviting two strangers to lodge with him (Genesis xix, 1, 2), and prescribed as a duty (Hebrews xiii, 2). When Jesus was in Jericho he told Zacchaeus, a tax gatherer, who had climbed a sycamore tree to see him, that he must stay at his house that day; and we are told that Zacchaeus 'made haste, and came down, and received him joyfully' (Luke xix, 1–6). When he went up to Jerusalem he probably stayed with Lazarus, Martha and Mary, who lived at Bethany, only a few miles away, and when he sent seventy of his followers to preach the gospel and heal the sick he told them to take nothing with them, but to rely on the hospitality of those dwelling in the towns they visited (Luke x, 1–12).

It is clear that there is very little here that we can call on to guide us in our efforts to cope with the strains and stresses of modern life. Many people would say that they would be glad to discard some of the burdens they have to bear. It may be, indeed we must hope that it will be, the case that when we begin to build the kingdom of heaven on earth, we shall greatly simplify our lifestyle, enabling us to adopt the life of Christ as a model. This does not mean we shall spend our time travelling and preaching, but that we shall find it possible to take no thought for the morrow and to leave the morrow to take thought for the things of itself (Matthew vi, 34). But the day when we can take this precept as a guide is not yet; it probably lies many centuries or even thousands of years in the future.

It may, however, be argued that, even if the daily life of Jesus is an inadequate guide to how we should conduct our lives today, we have no excuse for wrongdoing, because we have (uniquely) been given the faculty of conscience, and many people would claim that conscience should be given precedence over all other influences, even over the law. They would say that conscience enables us to know the difference between right and wrong and should in all cases be our guide. But in fact conscience is a very fallible guide and many atrocities have been committed in its name. The Inquisitors believed that they were being guided by conscience when they condemned Jews and heretics to be burned at the stake, and those who tried and either drowned or burned women accused of witchcraft also believed that they were acting in accordance with the dictates of conscience. Many moral issues could be cited on which conscience gives no clear guidance or on which people's consciences are divided. The fact is that what our consciences dictate is not based solely on strict moral absolutes, but is largely determined by what we are taught as children and what are the prevailing views of the society and more particularly of the circle of friends and acquaintances in which we choose or are forced by circumstances to live.

The fact that right and wrong are not always clearly ascertainable is not the only difficulty inherent to the 'test' theory, i.e. that the *sole* purpose of our life on earth is that we should undergo a test which we either pass or fail. Another difficulty is that we do not know how much is required of us to pass the test. We know that when we sin, that is to say when we break one or more of the Commandments or when we fail to live up to the requirements set out in the twenty-fifth chapter of Matthew's gospel (see page 2), we make a contribution towards failure; and that when we repulse Satan and resist his temptations or when we sincerely repent of a sin we have committed, we make a contribution towards passing the test. But we are not told what the pass-mark is. We know that it must be less than 100 per cent because no one can be perfect, and we are reasonably certain that it is not as low as zero, although there are some texts from which a different conclusion could be drawn. Thus John tells us that Christ is the propitiation for our sins, and not for ours only, but also for the sins of the whole world (1 John ii, 2), and Paul tells Timothy that God will have all men to be saved and to come unto the knowledge of the truth (1 Timothy ii, 4). Nor do we know what allowance will be made for factors affecting our behaviour over which we have no control.

A third difficulty is that we are not told clearly what the nature of the test is, or what rewards and penalties attend on our passing or failing it. On both these questions the New Testament gives us no clear guidance. In the simile used by Christ of separating sheep from goats (Matthew xxv, 31–46), we are given to understand that the test is our behaviour to our fellow human beings, especially to those in need or distress; the reward for those who pass this is inheritance of the kingdom prepared for them from the foundation of the world (verse 34) and eternal life (verse 46). The fate of those who fail is to be cursed, to be cast into everlasting fire, prepared for the devil and his angels (verse 41) and everlasting punishment (verse 46).

Other passages, however, give different versions. Is the reward for those who pass the test admission to the kingdom of God? If so, we find from John iii, 3 and 5, that the criterion is that we should be born again, and that the second birth must be 'of water and the Spirit'. Or is it the gift of eternal life? The same chapter of John's gospel tells us that whoever believes in Christ as the Son of God will not perish but will have eternal life (John iii, 16). Peter tells us that those who endure bodily suffering are free from sin (1 Peter iv, 1) and have therefore presumably passed the test. In another passage we are given the impression that salvation depends on the quality of life we enjoy on earth. Those who live in penury and hardship will be received into heaven, but those who enjoy riches and luxury will be denied salvation (Luke xvi, 19–31). All three synoptic gospels also record Christ as saying that 'it is easier for a camel to pass through the eye of a needle than for a rich man to enter the kingdom of God' (Matthew xix, 24; Mark x, 25; Luke xviii, 25). Warnings against the risks of spiritual pollution by riches and of trusting in wealth for salvation are given repeatedly in both the Old and the New Testaments: see, for example, Job xxxi, 24, 25; Psalm lii, 7; Proverbs xi, 28; Matthew vi, 24; Luke xii, 21; xvi, 13; 1 Timothy vi, 17; James i, 10, 11. Christ's apparently harsh and uncompromising statement would seem to render riches or even the pursuit of wealth an absolute bar to salvation. When, however, his disciples expressed astonishment at its severity, he qualified it by saying that 'with God all things are possible' (Matthew xix, 26).

All these difficulties, formidable though they are, may possibly be overcome if we are given further understanding, and the means of reconciling them may be revealed to us in due course. We do indeed expect that further revelation will be made at the appropriate time, for Christ has told us that 'the Comforter' (or Paraclete) 'which is the Holy Spirit, whom the Father will send in my name, he will teach you all things' (John xiv, 26).

But the fourth and final difficulty cannot be easily overcome. This is that the test theory depicts God in a very unfavourable light. For it would seem to be a capricious, pointless and even cruel act to create a race of sentient beings solely for the purpose of subjecting them to a test, and to condemn to eternal punishment those who fail to pass the test. If a man were to construct a number of models of himself and to equip them with electronic and mechanical devices to enable them to perform certain tasks, and if he were then to consign to the flames those models which failed to come up to his expectations, we should regard him as at least eccentric. If he were also able to endow those models with sentience and the ability to feel pain, so that their 'punishment' involved torture, we should accuse him of wanton cruelty. If, further, he were knowingly to ensure that the equipment in the models is faulty, so that their ability to perform the acts required of them is seriously impaired, we should regard him as a monster.

This, however, is a reasonably accurate analogy of the theory that the sole purpose of our creation is to impose on every individual the task of procuring his or her own salvation by passing a test. For the equipment with which we have been provided is imperfect, and the fact that it is *necessarily* imperfect (because all created beings must be less than their Creator) does not detract from the apparent injustice involved in the theory.

The test is not a test of knowledge but of behaviour and of response to God. It is generally held (by Protestants, at any rate) that we are required to pass, or fail, the test during our life on earth, and for this purpose we are given bodies, minds and souls. The task of our souls is to formulate objectives for the conduct of our life on earth, and to persuade or even compel our minds to accept those objectives. The task of our minds is manifold, but in this connection it is to reach decisions as regards our behaviour; these decisions will be based partly on the demands of our bodies, partly on the structure of our minds themselves and the ideas which they generate, and partly on the objectives imposed on them by our souls; the task of our bodies is to give effect to those decisions in speech and action.

It is clear that the test theory would have no meaning unless we were endowed with free will. This resides in the soul, which is free from constraint by God and enjoys this freedom because it does not rely on God for its maintenance in being. When the soul of an individual person is created, it is launched on its pilgrimage without further interference by God, except in so far as it sincerely seeks his help, and remains in being until God deliberately destroys it by a positive act, which he most certainly would not wish to do, and would in fact do only in the most exceptional circumstances, in which he judged that his will was being irremediably frustrated. In other words, it has eternal being, a mode of being which it shares with the angels. Our bodies and minds, on the other hand, have temporal being; their existence depends on continuous sustaining activity by God, who not only maintains them in being but also ensures that their behaviour conforms to the laws he has laid down for the governance of the universe, except in so far as it is controlled by the souls which he has implanted in them.

It is because we have souls that we are persons, distinct from all other living creatures, and the responsibility for our development, both as individuals and as a species, resides in our souls. It is also because we have souls that God is able to subject us to a test, and that we are able, with his help, to pass the test. However, our souls, being created, are imperfect, and our bodies and minds, through which our souls act, also fall short of perfection, not through any fault attributable to us but simply because they are created. It is true that by virtue of their freedom this inbuilt imperfection can be increased or diminished by the activity of our souls – this is indeed implicit in the test theory – but it cannot be entirely overcome.

Our bodies are indeed fearfully and wonderfully made (Psalm cxxxix, 14), but they are weak and fragile, liable to injury and disease, and subject to inevitable death after a life which is all too short for us to grasp the full nature of our duties and of the purpose we are required to serve. Our minds are also fearfully and wonderfully made but, like our bodies, they are subject to various diseases, such as depression, paranoia, schizophrenia, phobias and obsessions of many kinds, and they are also susceptible to disorders resulting from bodily diseases. In cases of bodily injury they are capable, in conjunction with our nervous systems, of experiencing pain to a degree far in excess of what is required to preserve life or to avoid danger. They can harbour illusions, some of which may be harmful, physically or morally, or both, and of course they are easily misled by Satan, whose handiwork they are often slow to recognise.

It is with this bodily and mental equipment, which is intricate and wonderful, but also woefully frail and imperfect, that we have been thrust into the world by God. It is a world which we believe has been created by God and must therefore reflect and reveal some part of his essence. Being created, it cannot reveal God fully, but as it is continually changing it reveals different aspects of the divine nature at different times; thus enabling us to understand God more fully. On the other hand, it is full of contradictions which confuse and frustrate our efforts to understand it. It is an incredibly beautiful world, and yet displays forces that are violently antagonistic to life – earthquakes, volcanoes, hurricanes, typhoons, avalanches, tidal waves and lightning, and other features less violent but equally destructive, such as pathogenic bacilli, bacteria and viruses.

When we come to examine the living world, we find that it is characterised by two motivating forces, interdependence and competition. The former is manifested in the fact that plants and animals rely on each other to ensure their mutual survival – the bee could not survive without the flower to provide honey, and many species of flower would not survive unless there were birds or insects to distribute their pollen. On a larger scale, the vegetable and animal kingdoms need one another to maintain the proper balance of oxygen and carbon dioxide (and other gases) in the atmosphere. Moreover, the vegetable kingdom is the basic source of all food for animals and itself depends on animal waste products to maintain the fertility of the soil.

The spirit of competition is manifested in the principle of natural selection, which has been in operation since life first appeared on earth, and which ruthlessly exterminates those members of a species that fall short of the qualities needed for survival, and equally ruthlessly exterminates species that fail to have the equipment necessary to cope with the changing circumstances in which they have developed. We human beings, in common with all living creatures, are endowed with instincts (or, if instincts are wholly psychical, with physical reactions) impelling us to preserve the species to which we belong and our individual lives as members of that species. And we find, when we reach an age at which we can assume the necessary responsibility, that we have to devote much of our time, our faculties and our powers to those ends, in providing food, clothing and shelter for ourselves and our dependants, and in caring for and training those of our dependants who have not yet reached that age.

The revelation of God we are thus given by the world and the living creatures in it cannot be opposed to God, it cannot contradict his nature; we know therefore that the world is not a vessel in which evil resides, except in so far as we ourselves have modified or polluted what God has made. For, as the story of the Garden of Eden tells us, evil did not enter the world until men and women fell from grace and allowed Satan to damage their souls and through them the environment in which they had been placed. We may say, paraphrasing Newton's first law of motion, that every part of the world (and of the universe) remains in the passive state in which God created it, or evolves in accordance with the laws implanted in it by God, except in so far as it is disturbed, or caused to diverge from those laws, by beings endowed with free will. On earth we are the only beings thus gifted; we alone have the power to *decide* to change the reflection of God which the world provides. For although we have an affinity with other animals whose bodily equipment matches ours and who also have minds – though these are very much less complex than ours – we have, in addition, been given souls, which can admit God or shut him out, and our souls are endowed with free will, whereby we can allow him to guide our lives or rebel against him and his creation.

Not only is this world a world which appears to depict God in contradictory terms, thereby confusing us and weakening our resistance to temptation, it is a world in which Satan roams freely 'like a roaring lion, seeking whom he may devour' (1 Peter v, 8). Satan's object is of course to frustrate God's plan for the human race and for the universe, and to achieve his end he whets all those appetites and desires which are contrary to God's will; in other words, he is constantly trying to induce us to sin, and being wily beyond belief employs every possible device to bring success.

But this is by no means the full extent of his powers. These are not limited to tempting us to do wrong. We can, with God's help, resist temptation, but Satan also uses the even more powerful weapon of deceit, against which we find it difficult to fight, since we do not recognise that it is being used. For Satan has the ability to masquerade as an angel of light (2 Corinthians xi, 14), persuading us to believe that what is really evil is good, and to act on this false belief. By this and other deceits he corrupts our souls into choosing and aiming at false objectives, and perverts our minds by implanting in them false beliefs. He, and other angels who with him rebelled against God and were cast out from heaven, carry on this evil work not only directly, but also by using as their agents gifted human beings who are striving to discover God's purpose and his will but, being corrupted by Satan, prophesy falsely and become misleading apostles and confidence tricksters while persuading us that they are agents of righteousness (2 Corinthians xi, 13–15). He has done this so convincingly that even those who are most favoured by God are deceived (Matthew xxiv, 24).

Several examples of this aspect of Satan's activity could be cited, but one will suffice to show how easily we, and those to whom we look to be our spiritual and our political leaders, are deceived. For he has persuaded us that the ultimate well-being, and even the salvation, of humankind will be attained by increasing to the maximum the production and distribution of wealth, and we, believing this end to be right, are assiduously pursuing it, although Christ has told us very clearly that it is a false objective (Matthew vi, 19, 20) and Paul has confirmed it (1 Timothy vi, 10).

If the test theory is true and is held to provide a complete description of God's purpose, we would have to believe that, having imperfections and frailties for which we are not wholly responsible, and being unceasingly assailed by an enemy who has an almost infinite capacity to deceive us, luring us from the right path, we will be punished by being cast into outer darkness, where there will be weeping and gnashing of teeth (Matthew viii, 11, 12; xiii, 41, 42, 49, 50; xxiv, 45–51; xxv, 14–46; see also Matthew xviii, 7–9; xxii, 11–14; Mark ix, 43–48). We cannot dismiss these warnings, for if the record of the evangelists is accurate they are the words of Christ himself. But it is clear that something is missing, for as they stand they cannot be reconciled with the truth that God is loving and compassionate, and that he gave his only begotten Son to expiate our sins. It is clear, therefore, that the test theory is inadequate to account for our existence and all that our existence entails, and that our duty to God requires us to ask how it should be supplemented.

The basis of the test theory is, as we have seen, the idea that God's sole purpose in creating humankind was that some members (possibly a large majority) of these created beings should achieve salvation and eternal bliss, the remainder being condemned to eternal punishment. There is, however, another theory, based on the same foundation, which has some similarities with the test theory; this is the theory of predestination*. Like the test theory, it is not wholly false, but it is incomplete and certainly misleading, and in my opinion it depicts God in an even more unfavourable light than the test theory.

This theory states that those who are to be saved were predestined to salvation before they were created, and those who are to be condemned to eternal punishment were likewise predestined to that fate. This belief, which is held by many Calvinists, is based on certain passages in Paul's letters to the Romans and to the Ephesians (Romans viii, 28, 29; Ephesians i, 4, 5, 11, 12), but is obviously incompatible with the fact that we have free will, for if our will is predestined to oppose the will of God so persistently that we are condemned to eternal punishment it is meaningless to say that it is free. If, on the

---

*Strictly speaking, what is discussed in this and the following paragraphs is the doctrine of 'election'. This theological doctrine is, however, an essential element in any theory of predestination, and as the latter term is more familiar to the general reader I have used it throughout, except once on page 19.

other hand, our will is not predestined, whether to serve God faithfully or to oppose him unwaveringly, but its ultimate fate is predestined however rightly or wrongly it exercises its freedom, the inescapable conclusion is that God is monstrously unjust.

We cannot lightly dismiss Paul's testimony. His unshakeable belief that only in Christ can we obtain salvation, his wholehearted and unceasing commitment to preaching the gospel, his courage in seeking converts and establishing churches even where his teaching was regarded as subversive, and his endurance under persecution and torture (2 Corinthians xi, 24, 25) must inspire us with awe and admiration, and must also lead us to give great weight to his interpretation of the gospel. We must certainly examine it closely to ensure that we do not misunderstand it, but at the same time we must recognise that he was not infallible, and that his teaching is, in some passages, coloured by the fact that he believed that the second coming of Christ to judge the world was imminent. This led him to dismiss as irrelevant any long-term commitment to the future, and to say that he would like all men to be celibate (1 Corinthians vii, 8, 38). Again, his insistence on the fact that 'the flesh' is continually at war with the Spirit (Romans viii, 4, 5, 8, 9, 12, 13; Galatians v, 13, 16–25; vi, 8) and must be ruthlessly subdued suggests that he was not immune from the dualist heresy, which became very prevalent in the second century, that the world was created evil. (In order to avoid the implication that Paul might be thus misguided, some recent versions of the New Testament translate the Greek word *sarx* not as 'flesh' but as 'sinful nature' or 'unspiritual nature', but his advice to reject the world, which is found in all his epistles, is evidence that the implication is not wholly false.)

Another ground on which a theory of predestination may be built is the belief that God, being omniscient, has complete foreknowledge of the future, including knowledge of who will be saved and who will be damned. But this argument is equally incompatible with the fact that God is just. Of course foreknowledge of a coming disaster which will give rise to great suffering does not imply evil in the person who has made the forecast, unless that person has played some part in causing the disaster. But God's role in predestination is not limited to his knowing in advance that evil will enter the world and that some predestined people will oppose his will so persistently that they will be condemned to eternal punishment; he has deliberately created the world and the human race in this way, and this cannot be reconciled with his goodness. It is of course admitted that God, in creating the world, knew from the beginning that the world, though good, would be imperfect and that human beings would sin; this fact does not detract from his goodness, but if he knew, before creating a particular human being, that that human being's sins would be so great as to merit eternal punishment, then he ought to have had second thoughts and refrained from creating that person. On the other hand, if he created that sinful person for some obscure reason related to the working out of his purpose, then he should be willing to bear the punishment for the sins committed to his advantage. Indeed this is precisely what he did by Christ's death on the Cross, but this fact contradicts the doctrine of election as a constituent of predestination.

The defence of a theory of predestination based on God's omniscience, if this is held to include his complete foreknowledge of the future, is also incompatible with the fact that we have free will. It is true that St Augustine of Hippo (in *De Libero Arbitrio*) set himself the task of persuading his friend Evodius that God's foreknowledge of the future and man's freedom were not irreconcilable, but his argument is based on the premise that God is omniscient. Very few people who are not atheists would be prepared to say that this premise is false. I suggest that the solution to the problem thus posed is that the meaning of the premise is not simple. God's omniscience is bound up with and is dependent on his omnipotence. It is general, not specific. God knows that his purpose will ultimately be fulfilled and he knows that we, the human race, will fail to recognise what that purpose is and will therefore from time to time act in such a manner as to frustrate it. He does not know in detail how any one person will orient his or her will, or how the human race as a whole will orient the communal will, whether in accordance with or in opposition to his will. But he can foresee the consequences of all such possible thelematic determinations and, whatever these may be, he can and will intervene when necessary to ensure that his will shall ultimately prevail.

Thus, if by predestination we mean that the ultimate fate of every individual soul is determined from the moment of, or even before, its creation it must, like the test theory, be rejected on the ground that it derogates from the goodness of God. It can, however, be given a wider interpretation, not open to objection on this ground, which will be explained later (see page 61). The conclusion to be drawn from the argument of this chapter is that all theories which start from the assumption that in creating the human race God had no purpose other than that of determining which members of it should be saved, or of giving them the opportunity to determine this issue by their behaviour, are incompatible with what we must believe is his nature. Moreover, by encouraging everyone to concentrate on the salvation of his or her soul, instead of on some larger objective, they are in conflict with Christ's warning that 'whoever seeks to save his soul will lose it and whoever loses his soul for my sake will find it' (Mark viii, 35). All such theories must therefore be discarded, and the following chapter will be devoted to outlining the framework of a theory which is not open to these objections.

2

The New Strategy

We know that God, having a will, also has a purpose, and that everything he does is done in furtherance of that purpose. The question posed on page 17 therefore leads to the more fundamental question: why did God create the human race and what tasks does he require it to perform? To answer these questions we must go back to one of the most basic statements in the Bible: 'God is love' (1 John iv, 8). John does not say that God loves, that loving is one of his many activities (though this of course is also true); he says that God *is* love. Love is the essence of his Personality. This is a profound statement and it is clearly our duty to try to discover its full meaning. This is not easy, because we use the word 'love' in many different senses, some of them quite trivial, as when we say to someone for whom we have no strong affection 'I'd love to see you tomorrow, but unfortunately I have another engagement. Perhaps some time later'. More usually we use the word to describe an emotional attachment to another person which may be but is not necessarily linked with sexual desire. We know, however, that although such an emotion may be very powerful, it does not express fully the meaning of love in its highest and purest form. This is that love which most nearly approximates to the essence of God; it is a spiritual activity, an emanation from our souls, an epiphany of the divine elements in our personality. It is in fact not an emotion, but an act of will. In saying this, however, it must be borne in mind that in its true sense 'will' is not an attribute of the mind whereby we force ourselves to do something we do not want to do or to refrain from doing something we do want to do, although in common speech it is often used in this sense. The motivating force in such cases is a counter desire, more powerful and sometimes lying at a deeper level than the desire (or the complex of desires) prompting the action or inaction. (Thus if someone desires to give up smoking, and maintains this resolve, it may be called an act of will, but is really the effect of a counter desire, stronger than the desire to smoke, e.g. the desire to avoid damage to one's health or the health of an unborn child.) In particular, when we speak of free will, we are not speaking of a mental faculty, but of a faculty of the soul, for free will means freedom from constraint by God, and this freedom is exercised by our souls, which are in direct contact with God, although it is in our minds that we have experience of it.

Love is not reflexive, it is outgoing and must have an object. We do, of course, love ourselves, in the sense that we do everything in our power to preserve ourselves and our identity, and to promote our well-being, but we do not experience an emotion of love for ourselves, an emotion of the kind with which we are familiar when we love another person. We are told to love our neighbour as ourselves (Leviticius xix, 18; Mark xii, 30), and this means that we ought to do everything in our power to preserve our neighbours and their identities, and to promote their well-being, even if we have no strong feeling for them, or even if we dislike them. We should not only behave in this way, we should desire to do so; loving behaviour to our neighbours should not be something we force ourselves to do to earn approbation from them or even from God, it should be the true expression of our character. Such undemanding love is the true meaning of the Greek word *agapé* (and the corresponding verb *agapao*), which is used exclusively throughout the New Testament where in English translations we find the world 'love' or 'charity'. Nowhere in all literature is the true meaning of 'love' described more clearly, more fully, or in more poetic language than in the thirteenth chapter of Paul's first letter to the Corinthians. It describes not only the love which we should bear to our neighbours, but also the love which is the essence of God's Personality.

Since God's love must have an object, the angels were created to be the recipients of it and to love him in return. The angels do not dwell in time and space, they are eternal beings dwelling in eternity. Although they are created they are co-eternal with God; this must be so, because there can never have been a moment in eternity in which they did not exist to be the recipients of God's love and to reciprocate it. Clearly the beings created by God to love him must be free to do so either wholeheartedly or only partially, or even to reject his love. If they were under a compulsion to love their creator, their love would be no more than a reflexion of his love, and to suggest that God's love is merely reflexive is blasphemous. The angels must therefore have free will, and this requires that their being shall be eternal being, not dependent on God's sustaining activity for its maintenance. Being created, however, they are necessarily imperfect, for only God is perfect; and being free, their imperfection takes on a positive form – in other words, they are sinful. No angel can respond fully to God's love and although some, typified by Michael, Raphael and Gabriel, approach perfection, even these are not faultless. Others, countless in number, are more sinful, falling far short of perfection; and being free, they are not constrained otherwise than by their own consciences and by the influence of the angelic society in which they have their being and live. We are told (in the twelfth chapter of Revelation) that Satan, envious of God's power, together with many other disaffected angels, rebelled and that there was war in heaven. Michael and his army of loyal angels fought against Satan and his followers, overcame them and cast them out from heaven, and with the freedom from angelic influence consequent on this expulsion Satan determined to use every device in his power to oppose God's will and to pervert his love, wherever it may be directed.

It is pointless to ask whether these events actually occurred. Events occur in time, and we are here dealing not with time but with eternity. The 'war in heaven' was not war as we understand it; the antagonists were not human or even material beings, they were spiritual beings and the weapons were spiritual weapons (cf. Ephesians vi, 10–16). We use the language of the world with which we are familiar because we have (at present) no other, but although earthly language is inadequate it can guide us towards understanding the truth. We need not doubt that the angels, including Satan, certainly exist, although their mode of existence is different from that of the world we see around us. Indeed, we human beings partly share their mode of existence, which is eternal being, although, as we do not know the angels through our senses, we are not normally aware of this fact. Being imperfect, the angels are spiritually defective and can experience emotions akin to envy and jealousy; we should have no difficulty therefore in accepting that some, led by Satan, carried those vices to the point of rebellion. Those angels who were not corrupted by Satan could not destroy him, nor could they prevent other angels from allowing themselves to maintain a link with him and, to a greater or lesser extent, to desire to follow his lead. They could, however, 'expel' him; that is to say, they could erect a spiritual barrier which he could not remove or penetrate, depriving him of the power positively to tempt those who had not fallen with him.

Clearly God could not allow this situation to continue. For he knew that Satan, now rendered even more vitriolically antagonistic by his expulsion, would redouble his efforts to frustrate the divine plan, and although he could not regain access to heaven in order to try to corrupt other angels, since the barrier excluding him cannot be breached from the outside (cf. Luke xvi, 26), he could be observed by those angels and they could, in their freedom, be seduced by what they could see, so that so long as Satan and his followers remained unredeemed and active, heaven could and would be corrupted by him. Satan's influence in heaven was therefore not entirely destroyed, but if the angels who had not been expelled with Satan sinned, it was (and is) not because Satan has power to tempt them but because the temptation arises from within, from their own sinful natures.

In order to rescue from destruction his plan for the ultimate governance of heaven by unalloyed and reciprocated love (agape) there were two options open to God. Either he could destroy Satan (and his followers) or he could devise means of redeeming him. We know that he rejected the first of these, and indeed it is not difficult to assign two reasons for this decision. The first is that God must be reluctant to destroy anything that he has created so long as any possibility of redemption remains. Indeed, since everything that God has created contains some element of his essence, God cannot destroy any of his creatures without destroying some part of himself, and therefore would not do so except in extreme circumstances, when no other course of action is possible. For we can be sure that self-destruction is not one of his characteristics. It may be argued that the death of a living creature contradicts this statement, but this argument is not valid. A plant or an animal dies when God ceases to pour forth the activity whereby its life had been maintained; the consciousness created by God and associated with the complexity which gives rise to its life and is inseparable from it (see page 49) is not destroyed, it is merely transferred to other creatures, not necessarily living. When human beings die, the consciousness inherent in their bodies is translated and added to the consciousness of their minds and both are preserved as elements of their personalities to do further work in bringing God's plan to fruition; moreover, their souls, which have eternal being, are not in any way altered. In no case, therefore, does death involve the destruction by God of any part of himself.

The second reason why God refrained from destroying Satan is that nothing would be accomplished by his doing so. For God knew that if Satan were destroyed, many disaffected angels who were unwilling to serve under Satan's leadership would take his place. They would do so with at least equal ferocity and determination, for they would regard God's contest with Satan as an unequal contest, arousing in them the same feeling of unfairness as we experience when we hear of a school bully knocking down a boy half his size. Direct action by God would therefore lead to a new rebellion, and the *status quo ante* would be restored.

God therefore, in his goodness, decided to devise a plan for the redemption of Satan, together with all his followers. This new plan would, of course, be subsidiary to, but would also contribute to and amplify, his overall plan to bring all created beings into harmony with him so that they may, without reservation, reflect his love. An important element in this subsidiary plan is that Satan's attention would be diverted. Instead of loitering outside the gates of heaven, where his evil presence could entice other angels to indulge in rebellious acts, his efforts to frustrate God's overall plan would be directed elsewhere. Thus God, while continuing to shower his love on all the angels, could leave the general administration of heaven to Michael and other loyal angels.

Obviously the redemption of Satan must be preceded by his defeat and, as we have seen, his defeat must be effected by creatures no higher in the hierarchical scale of being than Satan himself. Only thus could God ensure that no other disaffected angel would be tempted to follow Satan's example. And it is slowly being revealed to us that among the creatures on whom this formidable task is imposed, we, the race of human beings on earth, must be included. Elsewhere there may be others; if it is necessary for us to know about them the knowledge will no doubt be revealed to us at the right time. Moreover, as Satan and his followers constitute an army and carry on their war with God by means akin to military strategies, the forces arrayed against him must also be marshalled in military formations. Thus the human race must be regarded as an army, or at least as a battalion in an army, dedicated to waging war on him on one or more fronts. To fulfil our destiny, therefore, we have to be trained as an army, highly disciplined and under God's command, ready to obey his orders, however difficult compliance with them may appear to be. We must strive to understand as much of God's strategy as our finite minds can grasp, but our main role in his army is operational and tactical; we cannot, and are not expected to, comprehend in full or in detail how God will act to bring about the consummation of both his subsidiary and his overall plans. But everyone has his or her part to play and all are of equal value in the sight of our Commander-in-Chief. In general our duty is to try to understand our particular roles and to perform them to God's satisfaction. To this end we must aim at moulding our individual characters and directing our evolution in such a way that our desires conform with our duty and that we are ready to seek the grace of God to enable us to give effect to those desires. We must accept that this will involve sacrifice, but we must not allow the sacrifice to be a deterrent. As Paul told Timothy 'Endure hardship like a good soldier of Christ Jesus' (2 Timothy ii, 3). Our courage will be sustained by the knowledge that with every battle won in the war against Satan the burden will be lightened.

In order to create such an army on earth (and such other armies elsewhere as may be necessary) God embarked on a project so vast, so complex, and so imbued with the capacity to develop along lines that would embody his own characteristics of truth, beauty and goodness that in contemplating it our reaction can only be one of wonderment and awe. In comparison with the majesty of this project, our apparent relative insignificance would seem to rule out our playing any important part in it; thus our first reaction is to echo the psalmist's question 'When I consider thy heavens, the work of thy fingers, the moon and the stars, which thou hast ordained; what is man, that thou art mindful of him? and the son of man, that thou visitest him?' (Psalm viii, 3, 4). At the same time we are called upon to grasp the almost incredible fact that, on earth, we are the culmination of the project. When we fully understand this we are led, in humility, to recognise the magnitude of the honour that God has conferred on us in creating us to be soldiers in his army.

The steps taken by God to bring this new project into effect are summarised in the first chapter of the Book of Genesis, but the account given there does no more than provide us with a broad outline. It is left to us to fill in the detail and, by constant study and reference back to God for enlightenment, to discover the full extent and content of the strategy and what part we play in it.

The first step was the creation of time and space, matter and energy (let there be light), these last two being interchangeable in certain circumstances. It must be emphasised that all these are created and have temporal being; they are therefore quite unlike eternity, which is not created but streams out incessantly (or in theological terms *proceeds*) from God, a fact that was well understood by mediaeval theologians but is largely ignored today. This is regrettable, for our outlook on life, both in the present and in the here-after, is greatly enriched when the distinction between time and eternity is fully grasped. Even if time and space had never been created, eternity would have been a reality as an emanation from God and as a medium for being and for life; that is to say, for *eternal* being and *eternal* life, which are to be distinguished from temporal being and temporal life (see page 13).

We do not know when time and space were created; the current scientific theory is that they originated in a 'big bang', but the evidence as to when this occurred is contradictory. It is possible (though in my view improbable) that, like the angels, they are co-eternal with eternity and therefore with God, and that time stretches back endlessly into the past. If this is in fact the case, we should have to suppose that the universe has shrunk to a point and expanded to its maximum size cyclically an infinite number of times since its creation. However, we do not, and probably cannot, know whether this hypothesis is correct, and although speculation on it is interesting, it bears only indirectly on the question why God created human beings and the nature of their duty to him.

When God created time and space, matter and energy, all of which have temporal being, he implanted in them laws whereby they would interact. Time is linear and irreversible. It involves the concepts of before and after, earlier and later, and these cannot be interchanged (although the *perception* of sentient beings as to the order in which two events occur may differ). Matter and energy exist in space and time and, in accordance with the divine laws, interact with them. Thus change is inseparable from the created universe – in other words, the universe is not static – in obedience to the laws of God it evolves.

The next stage in the new strategy was the creation of life; that is to say, of temporal life, as distinct from eternal life, which is the mode of life of the angels and was created 'in the beginning', co-eternally with them. The insatiable curiosity of the human race has led many people to speculate on the origin of life on earth. Some have suggested that, in the primitive form of viruses, it was brought here by asteroids or meteors, implying that it existed, and probably still exists, elsewhere in the universe; this assumption, however, leaves the question of the origin of life unanswered. Others suggest that life arose as the inevitable consequence of the operation of the laws governing the physical universe. On this last assumption life must emerge if circumstances bring together certain elements in the appropriate surroundings and at the appropriate temperature. If this assumption is true, then, theoretically, it lies within the power of scientists to reproduce those circumstances and thereby to create life. In fact, even more bizarre claims have been made. To quote from an article on the doubly helical structure of DNA by Matt Ridley, published in *The Times* on 4 September 1995: 'Life, it transpires, is information. It is no more and no less than a potentially infinite message written in a simple linear code on a spiral staircase in twenty-one different kinds of three-letter words made up from a four-letter alphabet. Life is the consequence of the fact that the message can get itself copied. Two sentences – that's all it takes to describe.' The inadequacy of this definition is, however, obvious. Human life is not only information, it also embodies purpose. And as the precursor of and the accompaniment to human life, the same must be true of all life.

The theological position which must ultimately prevail is that temporal life was introduced into the universe by a specific act of creation by God, or perhaps by a succession of such acts. Even if it is accepted that the appearance of life was an inevitable consequence of the laws of evolution implanted in the universe at the time of its creation, it still remains true that the hand of God was involved in designing those laws in such a way as to incorporate this consequence, and because of its central importance the creation of life can be designated as a separate act. This act, or the first of a sequence of such acts, may not have taken place on earth – indeed, our understanding of the insignificance of the planet on which we live in comparison with the immensity of the cosmos might lead us to conclude that life on earth is only one instance, out of many millions, of this stupendously important development in the working out of God's strategy (see pages 64–65 and chapter 5). However, speculation on the possible diversity of the forms in which life may appear elsewhere in the universe, and on the distribution of those forms, does not concern us in our endeavour to discover our own purpose and destiny. But we should not dismiss this urge for knowledge as unimportant, or as being contrary to God's will; it may be that at some later stage in our development we shall be called upon to be involved with living beings in other parts of the universe (see pages 137–38 and 147).

It is part of our present task to study the appearance of life on earth and to discover the meaning, in relation to God's plan, that we can derive from that study. Interest in and the study of biology is therefore in accordance with the will of God; recognition of its importance is indeed part of our obligation to him. This task, however, is not imposed; it must be undertaken voluntarily. But, like all tasks, it involves duties which we are obliged but not compelled to perform. These include duties which require immediate attention and duties whose performance forms part of our pattern of living. The obligations involved in the former are usually of a type requiring individual action or action by a small group of people; those involved in the latter rest on the human race as a whole and are normally not confined to a short period but are extended over the whole of time. Of the latter type, one of the most important is the preservation, so far as lies in our power, of the living species which God has caused to evolve on earth by the operation of the laws he has devised to govern the development of the universe in time. For 'God saw everything that he had made, and, behold, it was very good' (Genesis i, 31). We are not debarred from killing plants and animals for our food, or to take steps to prevent our supply of food from being consumed or destroyed by other creatures, for we know that God has himself so ordained the evolutionary process that these practices take place among other species. Nor is it wrong, in present circumstances, to attack and destroy bacilli, bacteria or viruses which cause disease in human beings, or in plants or animals, although we may expect that, as the war with Satan progresses towards victory, other methods of preventing or curing human disease will be found (see pages 138–42). It is, however, our duty to adopt methods of farming whereby the control of pests is, as far as possible, effected by reliance on the forces enshrined in the divine laws governing life whereby the balance of nature is preserved. We are, of course, debarred from wanton killing and from practices, based on greed, which lead to the extinction of an entire species. These practices are sinful and will be punished, although the punishment may not fall on those who commit the sins but on future generations. It is indeed our duty to preserve all God's creatures, both animate and inanimate. If God is reluctant to destroy anything that he has created, we should certainly not act in any way that might conflict with this aspect of his will. The implications of the duties thus laid on us are immense. Paul reminds us that, from the beginning, the divine nature of God, and his invisible powers, are revealed to us in what he has created (Romans i, 20). And we may also bear in mind the words of Coleridge:

> He prayeth best, who loveth best
> All things both great and small;
> For the dear God who loveth us,
> He made and loveth all.

The laws governing the evolution of the universe are not only self-consistent, they also embody a final cause; that is to say, they are directed to an objective. This objective dwells in the will of God, and its fulfilment lies at the end of time. The urge towards its fulfilment, however, inheres now in all the matter of the created universe, and is maintained there by virtue of the fact that the universe, and all the matter in it, have temporal being and are preserved by the continuous sustaining activity of God who imparts this directional force through the medium of the laws by which every particle and wave-function is governed.

When the first living beings appeared on earth by the implantation of a new manifestation of God's creative power, this driving force, which I have elsewhere called 'the telos', was given a new dimension and a greatly enlarged role, containing the seeds of certain aspects of instinctive behaviour. It must be emphasised that the telos is not merely a concept, or a word used to describe certain modes of behaviour. It is a real entity, having temporal being. It is an indwelling force in the laws of the universe and in the physical reality which those laws control. In the enlarged form in which it activates living matter it becomes specific as well as general; it is directed to immediate ends as well as to an objective at the end of time. It implants in living matter new laws of evaluation to supplement the laws of development in time already present. It introduced, though gradually, the overwhelmingly powerful force of self-preservation. Life, once created, was animated by a driving urge to ensure that it would not be extinguished, but would continue to grow and diversify. This urge at first operated on units of living beings, displaying itself in each unit as an instinct to preserve its own existence; later, as distinct species began to appear, it enlarged itself to include the preservation of the species as well as that of the individual; later still, the preservation of the species took precedence, this priority being displayed in some species by the practice of destroying or isolating members of the species which were imperfect.

In the early stages the operation of the telos in living beings was entirely unconscious. The earliest forms of life acted in accordance with the new biological laws (interacting with physical laws), but were unaware that they were doing so. Nevertheless, with the passage of time living beings developed organs whereby they could react, in pursuit of the objective of self-preservation, to circumstances in the outside world at a distance from themselves, but this reaction fell short of any actual perception of those circumstances.

The situation was, however, completely changed and life was given new powers of development when God decided on the next stage in his strategy to defeat Satan. This was the creation of mind and its gradual linkage with the world of matter and energy. Again we do not know, and probably cannot know, when this act of creation took place; it is possible that the psychical world was created at the same time as the physical world, but that the two were held apart until God judged that evolution had progressed sufficiently for them to be brought together and allowed to coalesce and to interact. There are, of course, those who, as in the case of the creation of life, deny that any act of creation was involved in the appearance of living beings having powers of perception and therefore possessing minds to be the dwelling place of those experiences, but such views may be dismissed as being not only untheological but also unscientific. The business of science is to provide a rational explanation of facts, and there is, beyond any dispute or quibbling, a distinction between reacting to an external influence, e.g. the heat of the sun's rays, and actually experiencing the heat of those rays. Ice does not experience the feeling of warmth when it melts, nor does a malleable metal feel pain when it is beaten into shape. Admittedly these have no nervous system, but where this is present it is no more than part of the mechanism for mental experience; it is not the experience itself.

The expansion of reality brought about by the creation of mind was truly enormous. For it introduced the whole realm of experience, of consciousness, perception, emotion and desire. It is the dwelling place of a vast range of contrasting experiences, of liking and disliking, of love and hatred, trust and distrust, happiness and unhappiness, of pleasure, displeasure and pain, of pride and humility, of thankfulness and resentment, of the desire to serve others and promote their well-being, as well as of lust, anger and envy, of excitement and fear, exultation and distress, ecstasy and agony, and of joy and sorrow, delight and misery. It also introduced the power of belief, and of knowledge and understanding; it conferred the power of imagination and inventiveness; it provided a home for memories of the past and of hope for (or apprehension of) the future, and the appreciation of beauty in all its forms, the beauty of nature, of art and music and of words, and it laid the foundations for the understanding of language and of the abstract ideas of mathematics and philosophy. It also houses our moral sense and our understanding of right and wrong; moreover, although it could not from its own resources construct the categories of good and evil, it is able to provide a home for these when they have been introduced by God and, to a limited extent, to understand them.

This list of mental experiences and activities is no more than a brief summary; for a full understanding of God's handiwork and of our involvement in it we need further analysis. We start by noting that, although the creation of the physical world and the creation of mind were distinct acts of God, these two manifestations of his creative power are closely linked. Matter and mind both have temporal being (see page 13), though they differ in substance*, and each influences the other. The physical world and the psychical world are governed by laws ordained by God, and where they subsist in the same entity, as they certainly do in most living beings, and possibly also in non-living beings (see pages 47–48), these laws are supplemented by laws governing their interaction. Body and mind share the same nomothetic framework and constantly interact, and since this interaction is an essential feature of God's plan we must constantly seek his help in our efforts to understand it.

In fact, most mental experiences originate in and are caused by changes in bodily circumstances. The most obvious example of this interaction is the power of the mind to translate the physical stimuli reaching our brains through our sense organs into experiences of seeing, hearing, smell, taste and feeling. This power is at present incomprehensible and it is possible that we shall never understand it. The last three of these bring out particularly clearly the close interaction of mind and body.

---

*The original (and etymologically correct) meaning of this word denotes the underlying and unchanging reality in which the accidents, i.e. the observable (and in some cases measurable) appearances which are changeable, reside. In the physical world these include such matters as size, weight, hardness or plasticity (in solids), liquid or gaseous nature, colour, taste, temperature, etc. In the psychical world they include the whole range of mental experiences and faculties.

For in the case of smell, taste and feeling, the impact of the physical cause of the mental experience is direct and sometimes visible. If we enjoy the scent of a flower or the fragrance of a perfume or the taste of a savoury dish, or if we are repelled by a noxious odour or the taste of rotting meat, we can readily detect the chemical substances which act directly on our olfactory nerves or our taste buds. And if we enjoy the luxury of a warm bath or feel the pain of a blow or a torn ligament, the direct connection between the physical cause and the mental experience is obvious. In the case of hearing and seeing, however, the original physical cause is distant and has to be transmitted to our sense organs through a medium of which we are not directly aware, although, of course, it is discoverable by scientific analysis. We can see, as well as feel, the impact of a boot on our shin, but we cannot see the airwaves which convey to our ears the sound of a friend's voice or of a distant church bell, or the electro-magnetic vibrations which convey a landscape to our eyes.

In all cases, however, the physical circumstances which give rise to sensory perception have to be transferred from the point of impact to the brain by means of the nervous system, and it is when they reach the brain that the mysterious and inexplicable transition from a physical event to a mental experience takes place.

Another example of the close interaction of the physical and the psychical components of the created world is provided by the fact that the health or sickness of our bodies will in almost all cases affect our minds, and vice versa. Pain is a mental experience but always has a physical origin in the form of bodily injury or malfunctioning, even where this is not obvious, e.g. when one has a headache. Again, recovery from an illness will be aided by a hopeful attitude of mind and faith in the competence of one's physician, and will be impeded by a pessimistic outlook. Mental distress caused by bad news may give rise to weeping and, more generally, any psychological damage will usually display itself in abnormal bodily behaviour. We have some empirical knowledge of how this interaction works and are able to use this knowledge by prescribing drugs to alleviate depression or hyper-activity, but our knowledge is very sketchy and we must be careful not to abuse it. We have also become expert in the use of analgesics and anaesthetics, but in no case does our empirical knowledge throw any light on what actually happens at the junction of brain and mind, and it may be that this knowledge will forever be hidden from us.

The importance of the psycho-physical interaction involved in sensory perception for the survival of the individual, and also of the species to which it belongs, is obvious. To the extent that this is the case, the interaction may reasonably be regarded as the product of natural selection in accordance with Darwinian principles. But in human beings the experiences to which this interaction gives rise far exceed, in number, variety and intensity, those necessary for survival, or even those which enhance the values attached to survival and which might therefore, by an extension of the Darwinian theory, be aligned with sensory perception. For these additional experiences a reason must be assigned, and this can only be done by our accepting, as an irrefutable truth which no one is entitled to deny, that the immensely rich variety of experiences which we, the human race, enjoy, or by which we are distressed, is an essential factor in the performance of our duties as soldiers in God's army.

Among these additional experiences, transcending sensory perception but equally mysterious and no doubt equally important for the fulfilment of our destiny, is the enjoyment we derive from the contemplation of great works of art or the wonders of nature, and the power to appreciate the significance of great truths. The fact that these aspects of the world around us, and our power to appreciate their beauty, have their origin in God is rarely acknowledged, although we do, in some hymns, recognise that the beauty of nature which gives us so much pleasure is God's handiwork. We thankfully sing 'All things bright and beautiful, all creatures great and small; All things wild and wonderful, the Lord God made them all'. We also sing 'For the beauty of the earth, for the beauty of the skies ... Lord of all, to thee we raise, this our thankful hymn of praise'; and in a later verse of this hymn we get close to giving thanks, not only for the existence of beautiful things to give us joy, but also for the fact that, having minds, we are able to enjoy them. We recognise God's bounty by singing 'For each perfect gift of thine, to our race so freely given, Lord of all, to thee we raise, this our thankful hymn of praise'. But the fact that this bounty is an essential element in a very complex plan, devised before the beginning of time, for victory over Satan, needs to be not only recognised but constantly and loudly proclaimed. If this is not done our understanding of this plan can never be complete and the war with Satan will be prolonged.

Mental experiences can also be self-generating, as is evidenced by the power of imagination. A simple example is when we experience pleasure by imagining ourselves in a pleasurable situation, or when we experience fear by imagining ourselves to be threatened, although no actual danger impends. Imagination may not always be under control, as in the case of dreaming, and an uncontrollable imagination may also be a feature of certain psychological disorders, but it is important that a healthy mind, when awake, should be able to hold imagination in check and to direct it so that it does not clash with the will of God. In some cases self-generating mental activities can give rise to bodily reactions. Possibly the most important example of this phenomenon is to be found in the power of the mind to devise and create, or to draw from a source already created by God, new sights and sounds, or other forms of artistic expression, to delight us through our senses. Equally remarkable is the power to devise new philosophic systems or new insights into mathematical truth.

The appreciation and pleasure provided by our mental experiences, whether their source is self-generated or has a physical cause, are sufficient evidence of what God has done, and is doing, to ensure that our fight with Satan will be not only arduous but also enjoyable. Even more remarkable, however, is the fact that our minds also have the faculty, quite distinct from the power of appreciation and enjoyment, of formulating and understanding abstract ideas, and in particular of grasping the *concepts* of truth, beauty and goodness, which we recognise as being part of the essence of God and therefore as evidence of his existence. This power is an illustration of the mental faculty of comprehension or understanding. A further illustration of this faculty is our ability to grasp the concept of purpose, and to pose questions prompted by this concept. Thus we are not content merely to observe and enjoy the universe, both physical and psychical, which God has created, we also want to know how it works and why he has created it, and in particular why we have been created and how we can fulfil the purpose which our understanding tells us cannot be separated from our creation.

Closely allied to this faculty of conceptual understanding is the power to analyse the structure of language and the principles of logic. In association with our brains, our minds are the repository of knowledge, whether experienced or learnt, and of memories, which are stored in the brain (by a process which we do not fully understand) and which the mind can bring to the surface of consciousness when the desire or the necessity to do so presents itself. No other animal species has conceptual understanding but some, including certainly all those having a nervous system and a brain, can acquire knowledge and can store and use memories. Both these faculties, however, are governed by the telos and are therefore limited to purposes directly related to survival and propagation.

The transformation of physical events into mental experiences through the agency of our sense organs, the pleasure or pain to which those experiences give rise, and the power to generate concepts independently of any physical action do not, in human beings, exhaust the functions of the mind. All these are possible because our minds are in contact with the world of time and space, but they do not suffice for God's purpose. To achieve this, God has provided that our minds shall also be in contact with our souls, and thereby with eternity. It is our souls which reach the important decisions relating to our ultimate destiny; but these must be expressed in action, and for this purpose God has arranged that our minds shall act as intermediaries, transmitting the soul's instructions to the body. There is, however, an important distinction to be made between the mind's interaction with the body and its interaction with the soul. This is that the former is two-way, but the latter only one-way. The soul can causally influence the mind, but the mind can do no more then present to the soul facts and circumstances, beliefs and desires, on which the soul is entirely free to reach whatever decisions are most likely to further its own chosen objectives.

Through its link with the soul, the mind can become the dwelling place of the uniquely human attribute of conscience. Conscience is the gift of the Holy Spirit, and the soul has the power to reject this gift, although it rarely does so completely. Conscience is the faculty whereby we know that we ought to do what is right and eschew what is wrong; in other words, it is the spiritual faculty whereby we accept, though we cannot define, the concept of duty. Thus the existence of conscience implants in our minds the concepts of right and wrong as moral issues, not merely as synonyms for expedient and inexpedient. It is often claimed that conscience not only tells us that we ought to do what is right, it also tells us what actions (or thoughts) are right and what are wrong. In this, however, we have already seen (page 9) that conscience is a very fallible guide. Our ideas of what is right and what is wrong are not generated in our consciences but are mostly based on our genes, on what we are taught by our parents, on the opinions of our friends and colleagues, on all the experiences to which life exposes us and on what moral rules our souls generate and implant in our minds. Thus the content of the categories of right and wrong may differ widely between one person and another, between one tribe and another, between one nation and another, and from one century to another. The only general principle to which almost everyone would subscribe is that it is right to treat other people (and the members of other species) as we would wish them to treat us. It is worth noting that this precept (Matthew vii, 12) is common to all religions and is explicitly stated in the scriptures of most of them.

The fact that conscience is unique to human beings must be emphasised. For there are many people who would claim that it is to be found in other species, and would cite as evidence the fact that some animals can be trained to obey orders and, more convincingly, that cases have been cited where dogs have rescued their owners from danger even at the risk of their own lives. They can also point to the fact that many species display modes of behaviour that appear to correspond to a distinction between right and wrong (e.g. the instinct of a mother to protect her young). All these, however, are the result of natural selection and the urge of every individual to preserve itself and its species. They are instinctive and are not based on a moral sense. This applies even in the case of a dog endangering its life to save its owner. Naturally, many of these evolutionary modes of behaviour are to be found in human beings also, but our sense of right and wrong lies much deeper than the impulses that motivate other species to behave in a quasi-moral way, and has a different origin. For in addition to the moral sense which we apply in our daily lives we also understand, or at least admit the existence of, the categories of good and evil. We dimly recognise that these are absolutes and are more fundamental than the categories of right and wrong. With the concept of duty or obligation also implanted in our minds, we also know that we must learn to order our affairs and to direct our evolution in such a manner that 'right' tends to coincide with 'good' and 'wrong' with 'evil'.

The link binding our minds to our souls enables them to harbour and to give expression to agapeic love, the love which Christ commended to his disciples, which indeed he commanded them to show to one another (John xiii, 34; xv, 12). It also enables them to grasp the concept of eternity as an unbounded medium embracing, but immeasurably greater than, time and space. And it empowers us to believe in the existence of a spiritual dimension, a world which is very different from, and superior to, the world in which we live our earthly lives and is revealed to us through our senses; and to believe in the existence of, and in part to know, an infinite Being who is the author, origin and creator of everything that is.

The fact that we, and other creatures, have minds, the wide variety of uses to which this addition to their physical bodies can be put, and the contribution thereby made to the well-being and the survival of the creatures thus endowed, are visible for all to see. It may be asked, therefore, what is the point of this analysis of mental activities, with which everyone is familiar and which is in any case incomplete? The answer is contained in the question, or rather, the wording of the question suggests the answer. For this is that familiarity breeds neglect; we are so accustomed to the experiences which the creation of mind and its association with matter have brought into our lives that we ignore the fundamental truth they reveal. This is the incredible inventiveness of God in devising such a wonderful multiplicity of faculties and experiences and in endowing some of his creatures with those faculties and experiences and to be aware of having them.

For we must add to the list given in the preceding paragraphs what is perhaps the most fundamental experience of all, namely the experience of awareness, which has its lodging in consciousness, and particularly in self-consciousness. We are aware of our unique identity, and know that it is we who are experiencing the emotions generated by our minds or by the world around us, and otherwise using the mental faculties with which we are endowed. These truths are so wonderful and so utterly beyond our comprehension that we ought to be constantly reminding ourselves that they come from God, that what they reveal has been brought into being by God as part of his strategy for the defeat of Satan, and that it is our duty to keep these facts in the forefront of our minds so that we may use all our faculties to ensure the success of this strategy.

In the analysis of mental phenomena given in the preceding paragraphs emphasis has been laid on the range of faculties and experiences observable in human beings, and any reference to the mental powers of other species has been no more than incidental. The fact that the members of most, possibly all, animal species have minds and use them to enhance the interest and pleasure of their lives as well as to enable them to survive is, however, also important and must not be ignored. Three points must be made. The first is that the mental activities of animals have been developed by the laws of evolution alone, whereas in human beings those laws have in some cases been used as a mechanism only, the driving force being the operation of the human will. Nevertheless, some animals display, in a rudimentary form, characteristics which in human beings attain great importance. Chimpanzees use sign language to communicate with one another and some have been taught the sign language used in America by deaf and dumb people. They have learned a few hundred words in this language and have used them intelligently to communicate in a very simple way with human beings. Some animals have an elementary understanding of number, though few, if any, would be able to count beyond ten. It is probable also that no animal can abstract number from the articles being counted, so as to understand, for example, that three plus two equals five. Many species, especially birds, have an appreciation of beauty, either of colour and pattern or of sound, although this appreciation is limited to what is necessary for the preservation of the species.

Moreover, it must be acknowledged (lest we should become complacent) that other species possess instincts, powers and abilities, residing in or associated with their minds, which we have never possessed, or which we possessed at one time but are no longer in evidence. These may have been entirely lost or may be latent. Some of these faculties are not needed for the preservation of our species; others may have some value for this purpose but, not being essential, have been held in restraint by God lest we should misuse them, or have become submerged by the accumulation of intellectual and emotional experiences which we have developed to enhance the variety and pleasure of our lives. Among these faculties which we do not possess and do not understand, a remarkable instance is the homing instinct displayed by some animals. Cases have been cited where dogs have been taken more than a hundred miles from their home and left to fend for themselves, and after the lapse of some days or weeks have found their way home. The exceptional power of pigeons in this respect is well known, and is even used by human beings for sport or competition. A similar power possessed by salmon (and possibly other fish) enables them to swim back from a distant ocean to the river in which they were spawned. It is probable also that some species of animals have telepathic powers, which they use to communicate to other members of their species facts that are important for their preservation. But while admitting all these facts we can still rightly claim that our minds surpass in inventiveness and in variety of powers, to an immeasurable degree, those of any other species.

The second point to note is that, although as soldiers in God's army we obviously have a far more intimate and important role in the defeat of Satan than any other creature on earth, we should resist any temptation to preen ourselves on our superiority by reflecting that we, alone among God's creatures, have the power to dominate and, within limits, to control the telos, which is a God-given instrument for the success of his strategy, and have not always used this power wisely. Before the advent of the human race the activity of the telos was in complete harmony with the will of God and served to advance the cause of his strategy. When the Fall of man took place, however, as described allegorically in the third chapter of Genesis, this harmony was broken and has not yet been fully restored. From time to time attempts have been made to remedy this situation, but these have more often than not been misdirected; and even when some repair has been effected, the sinfulness of humankind has given rise to new breaches. For the wills of men and women have perverted the telos, as it dwells in them, leading them to adopt practices and ways of life that tend, not towards self-preservation, but towards self-destruction. Thus in the history of the human race the activity of the telos has been a mixture of harmony and discord.

The third point is that although the distribution by God of his gifts, both bodily and mental, among the different species which have evolved in accordance with his laws, is apparently very uneven, we may be sure that those gifts are distributed in due measure, according to what each species is required to contribute to the achievement of his purpose. We know this to be true because we know that God does not act capriciously or wantonly. He would not have devised such an intricate system, in which every part is properly adapted to the purpose assigned to it, unless the whole had been worked out in every detail in advance. This applies even to us human beings, who, having free will, can mar his handiwork, and are constantly doing so. This may appear to involve a contradiction; if all the details of God's plan have been worked out in advance, how can any interference by us modify it? The answer to this apparent paradox is that the detailed plan is flexible. It is so devised that any deviation from it leads to circumstances which will inevitably bring those who have deviated or have caused the deviation, or their descendants, back on course. God does not know in advance what deviations may take place, but his plan is so devised that any departure from it contains within itself the seeds of its own rectification. The operation of this inherent self-therapy may be very slow, but God is not in a hurry – as the psalmist says 'A thousand years in thy sight are but as yesterday when it is past, and as a watch in the night' (Psalm xc, 4).

The lesson we learn from this is that, although we rightly regard ourselves as the chief agents in the implementation of God's new strategy, we are not the only agents. All created beings, both living and non-living, have their appointed roles. In no circumstances, therefore, may anything that God has created be regarded as vile or of no account. If any living creature exists, and has come into being by the operation of God's laws alone and without interference by us, we may be sure that God has willed it so, and that all such creatures are seen by God as having value. Where we interfere – as of course God knows that we must, otherwise the exercise of our free will would be so limited as to be valueless – we must be certain that we are doing so in accordance with God's will and under his direction. There can, I think, be no doubt that the selective breeding of crops and domestic animals falls into this category, but it is very questionable whether the same can be said about genetic engineering. For in selective breeding, whether of plants or animals, we are doing no more than controlling and modifying the circumstances in which the law of natural selection operates; we are not interfering with the law itself. In the case of animals, domestication may be regarded as a highly sophisticated form of symbiosis – we feed the sheep and protect them from the wolf, and in return the sheep give us their wool to clothe us and their flesh for food. In genetic engineering, however, we are not only controlling circumstances, we are interfering with the mechanism devised by God for the maintenance and the propagation of life, and this is almost certainly contrary to his will.

We can understand, at least in part, why God has conferred on us the immeasurable riches which we enjoy as a result of the creation of mind. He has done so, not only to show his agapeic love for us, but also because our use and enjoyment of these riches are necessary for the success of both his subsidiary plan to defeat Satan and his overall plan to bring the whole of his creation (including the angels) into harmony with his will. It follows that we must use these riches as fully as possible, but while doing so we must also ensure that our enjoyment of them accords with his will. We know that he has also, to a lesser degree, conferred the same blessing on to other species and has done so for a specific purpose; it is therefore incumbent on us, as his chief agents, to be concerned with the extent to which mental faculties and experiences are distributed among his creatures and to discover the rational basis underlying this distribution, in the sure knowledge that he will reveal his secrets to us, so far as it is necessary for us to know them, in due time.

It is right, therefore, that we should make every effort to discover the range of mental activity in the living world and also whether mind plays any part in the evolution of the non-living world. We must build on what we know and try to be clear about where our knowledge is deficient. For we are sometimes too ready to claim certainty where we ought humbly to admit that we know very little. As I have already pointed out (page 33), we do not know when mind was created. We know very little about its structure and properties, about its relation to consciousness and awareness, about the laws by which its behaviour and manifestations are governed, the range over which and the extent to which God has imposed limitations on its powers of achievement, about how its substance differs from the substance of matter or about how, in spite of this difference of substance, matter and mind are linked in the same entities and constantly interact. On all these matters, if we are to be effective soldiers in God's army, we must strive, with God's help, to discover as much as he is willing at any time to reveal to us.

The importance of humility cannot be overemphasised. For in this field it is very easy, and very tempting, to assume that we have knowledge where in fact we are very ignorant. And, because we are here dealing with non-material entities which cannot be weighed or measured, it is difficult to prove that those who falsely claim to have such knowledge are in error. But we may be sure that God will not tolerate any misuse of these false claims, although the penalty in this world may not fall on those who are guilty of misuse but on others. One example must suffice. We believe that in human beings, and possibly also in animals with the most highly developed brains, there are at least two levels at which mind is functional – the conscious and the subconscious – but we know very little about the activity of mind at these levels. This deficiency in our knowledge, if not admitted by those in whom we place our trust, can be dangerous and in individual cases may be disastrous, as when psychoanalysts extract from the subconscious minds of their patients, fictitious memories of abuses inflicted on them in childhood. Because of the intangible nature of mind, the misuse of false claims to knowledge is a far greater danger in the treatment of mental disorders than in that of physical ailments. Those who engage in such treatment should bear in mind that, although in earthly life they may not suffer any ill consequences of the wrongful use of the trust placed in them, they will, at or before the end of time, have to answer to God for what they have done.

Reverting to our exploration into the range of mental powers and activities, it may be taken as certain that mind dwells in all the higher animals, and probably also in all animals having nervous systems and brains. It is, however, obvious that even in these the range of activities in which their minds engage is, in comparison with the human mind, very small and is limited to little more than those attributes which have a survival value in the continual struggle of the telos to preserve the life of the individual and the species to which it belongs. It is, however, possible that mind is also associated with the bodies of animals without nervous systems and if, as I think is probably the case, the telos in living beings dwells in the mind, we must believe that in some form mind is also a characteristic not only of all animals but also of trees and plants and other vegetable forms of life, and even in viruses. If this is the case we must, when studying the behaviour of living things (and viruses) take into account not only physical law but also the laws governing the activity of mind and its interaction with the bodies of those beings. It would then follow that, except in the case of human beings, the behaviour of all living creatures may properly be described as reflex action, extending the meaning of this term to include the deterministic activity of mind as well as that of matter.

As an example of the possibility that plants have minds it may be remarked that some people are convinced that they can encourage their plants to grow by talking to them, and this possibility should not be dismissed as a childish fantasy. Although it would seem to be certain that no plant can hear speech, it is possible that some or all plants can receive telepathic messages, and that it is to these that flowers respond when addressed with words of encouragement and love.

If in living creatures the telos dwells in the mind then, since it also inheres in the physical world, we are led inevitably to inquire whether mind and matter may be associated in non-living beings, in stones and clay and the waters of the ocean, in the sun and other stars, in black holes and in cosmic dust, and if so, what mental activities are possible for such beings. These questions are not fanciful or frivolous; they are being seriously asked by computer technologists today. It is even asserted by some that within the next twenty years it will be possible to construct a computer which will pass the Turing test. In this test a human being and a computer are placed side by side in a room and are interrogated by a person in an adjoining room who cannot see them. The interrogator asks questions which the human being and the computer are required to answer (even if the answer is 'I do not know'), and the answers are displayed on a screen. The questions are designed to enable the interrogator to decide which replies are given by the computer and which by the human being; if he fails in every case to do this with absolute certainty, the computer is held to have passed the test.

The possibility that inanimate matters can have some elements of mind is also of theological significance. We can already construct devices which relieve us of certain domestic tasks (e.g. washing machines), and more complex devices can, in a few seconds, perform arithmetical calculations arising in the course of very intricate mathematical operations. If it is also possible to construct electronic devices which can think and feel, and if we succeed in giving reality to this possibility, we could assign to such devices the responsibility for acts involving difficult moral decisions, thereby relieving ourselves of a responsibility which God intended us to take on our own shoulders. Such devices could have no moral sense other than that programmed into them, but if Satan were allowed to play any part in the programming, as is certainly possible, the consequences could be unimaginably evil. For this reason it is certain that God will not allow us to cross this threshold until we have evolved much further along the lines he has laid down for us.

The possibilities outlined in the preceding two paragraphs may be given a logical foundation and therefore also a more readily acceptable aspect if we adopt, with some modification, the ideas of the Jesuit thinker Pierre Teilhard de Chardin. The thesis is propounded in almost all his works, and especially in *The Phenomenon of Man* (Fount paperback, 1977), is that the basic psychical substance (in the true sense of this word, as explained on page 34) is consciousness. Consciousness must be clearly distinguished from awareness, which does not make an appearance until consciousness has reached a high level of complexity. Consciousness is atomic, and one or more atoms of consciousness are present in every elementary physical particle. Consciousness is also present in the telos, and part of the mechanism by which the telos seeks to attain its objective is an urge towards complexity. Thus an increase of complexity carries with it an increase of consciousness, and both are inherent in the structure and the laws of the physical universe.

From these simple ideas we learn that, in creating the universe of time, space, matter and energy, God ensured that elementary physical particles would have an urge to combine to form atoms and that the same urge would lead atoms to combine to form molecules which are the building blocks of living matter. At each stage the increase of complexity added a measure of consciousness to supplement the consciousness already present in the constituents of the more complex entity.

With the creation of life this process was carried further and accelerated. The simplest forms of life evolved to give rise to more complex forms, and at every stage in this process the consciousness inherent in the urge towards complexity was added to the total consciousness of the living beings engaged in that stage. In the early stages, when propagation took place by fission, the rate of increase of consciousness was small, since the increase in complexity consisted only in the replacement of one organism by two, but when propagation by the union of male and female elements developed, the rate increased rapidly, with the result that the total quantity of consciousness present in the higher animals is enormous. In these it approaches the level of awareness, the level at which it is manifested in human beings and which is the highest degree of complexity that consciousness can reach.

In human beings awareness itself has been further refined, for it has been taken over by the soul, so that in every man, woman and child there is not only mental awareness, which has temporal being and enables us to know by reason that God exists, but also spiritual awareness, which has eternal being and enables us to have direct experience of God's existence. Both types of awareness lead, by different paths, to our knowing that we are under an obligation to carry out God's will. It is of course possible to use the power of reason to deny the existence of God, and some people have done this using arguments which, though faulty, are believed by them to be valid. In such cases the spiritual awareness is repressed, giving rise to conflict, with damaging results to both the spiritual and mental constituents of their being. This conflict, if not resolved during early life, will certainly be resolved in the next stage of life, when the temporal being of mental awareness will be transformed by the soul into eternal being. Spiritual awareness will then become dominant, leading (though possibly only gradually) to a clear mental understanding of the rational grounds on which the existence of God rests and to fuller knowledge of his purpose in endowing us so richly.

If the ideas of Teilhard de Chardin are right, as I believe they are, then all mental faculties and powers of experience are complex organisations of psychical particles, analogous to, though differing from, the complex organisations of physical particles which make up the structure of the world in which we live. We may suppose that each psychical particle is endowed with a unit of consciousness and that in the complex structures which we recognise as mental experiences and activities, the total consciousness of the units of which the structure is composed is enhanced by the consciousness attributable to its complexity. Thus in the mental as well as in the physical universe the total consciousness of a complex organism is greater than the sum of the units of consciousness of the particles of which it is composed, the additional consciousness being attributable to the complexity of the organism, which itself is in many cases due to the operation of the telos.

In fact Teilhard de Chardin went further. From the fact that mental experiences are inseparable from consciousness – which, of course he distinguished from awareness – he *identified* the psychical particles with units of consciousness. Mind and consciousness cannot be distinguished; we should therefore say that all mental faculties and activities, and the powers of experiencing possessed by all minds, are complex organisations of units of consciousness. This leads to the conclusion that an element of mind exists in all physical particles and therefore in the whole of the physical universe, and that the creation of mind coincided with the creation of matter; in other words, that the first and third steps in God's new strategy, though quite distinct, since the substance of consciousness is different from that of matter, took place at the same moment in eternity. The possibility mentioned on pages 32–33 would be a fact.

The fourth and final stage in God's intricate and purposeful strategy has been foreshadowed, and has indeed been explicitly assumed to have taken place in all that has been said in this and the previous section. Nevertheless, it deserves particular attention and analysis. For it involved the union of spiritual entities, having eternal being and therefore free, with natural (i.e. physical and mental) entities, having temporal being and therefore not free, but subject to the physical, chemical, biological and evolutionary laws which God has built into all living creatures, and to the psychical and interactive laws which he has imposed on all those living beings which have minds. The union of spiritual and natural beings brought about by this stage in God's strategy involved the creation of new living beings, outwardly physical and part of the evolutionary chain, but endowed in part with eternal being; these creatures are of course ourselves, humankind, the only creatures on earth who are free to decide whether to ally ourselves with God or with Satan.

There has of course always been a link between the spiritual and the natural worlds: the sustaining activity of God whereby every physical entity, and also every psychical entity, is maintained in being, and whereby life – that is, *temporal* life – is maintained in every living creature*. By this activity also some element of the essence of God is imparted to the whole of the natural world. But this activity is a link, not an indwelling part, removable only by God, of the substance of those entities which make up the natural world, both animate and

---

*The activity required for the maintenance of being, that required for the continued existence of life and that required for the continued existence of mind are probably all distinct modes of God's expressing himself, but as we cannot know in what this distinction lies I shall disregard it and shall continue to use the word 'activity' in the singular.

inanimate. This link can be broken by God at any time by withdrawing his sustaining activity, and such a withdrawal occurs when an animal or plant dies. A distinction must, however, be made; the activity maintaining the *life* of a living creature is withdrawn instantaneously at the moment of death but the activity maintaining its *being* may be withdrawn only gradually. Thus if a domestic animal kept as a pet dies, the activity maintaining its being may be transferred from the animal itself to the memory of its owner and may not be totally withdrawn until that person dies.

The final stage in God's strategy differed from the earlier stages in an important way. In each of the first three stages God exercised his creative power once only. When he created time, space and the universe, he implanted in them laws whereby their future development has been governed without further intervention by him, apart from his activity to maintain them in being. Likewise when he created life and mind, a single act of creation was in each case all that was required. These were then transmitted from generation to generation by the laws of propagation and evolution inherent in them in their creation. But the final stage was not completed in a single act of creation; in order to make it effective God undertook the task of creating a new soul for every human being.

It follows that the death of a living being, whether a plant or an animal, does not conflict with the fact that God will not destroy anything that he has created (see page 25), unless this is necessary to avoid the frustration of his plan. Although God's sustaining activity and his creative activity have certain features in common, which sometimes lead us to confuse them, they are quite distinct. In the case of human beings, earthly death does not lead to the withdrawal of God's sustaining activity; the body and the mind are transformed (1 Corinthians xv, 44), and God's activity continues to sustain them in their new form. The soul, of course, having eternal being, continues to exist without being sustained by this activity.

The union of the natural and spiritual worlds in human beings, which constituted the final step in the creation of an army to fight Satan, completely altered the state of affairs prevailing before that step was taken. It is important to note that this step was absolutely necessary. God knew, before embarking on his new strategy, that he would have to take it and to accept all its consequences. For in order to avoid the adverse consequences of a defeat of Satan by God himself (as outlined on page 25) it was necessary to create a race of beings capable of making decisions and acting on them on their own responsibility. Such beings must be free from constraint by God and must therefore be endowed with a spiritual element dwelling in eternity and having eternal being. By virtue of their having this mode of being, these spiritual elements, the souls of human beings, are preserved and continue to exist, even after the earthly death of the body, without further activity by God or any intervention by him. They cannot be destroyed except by a positive act of God, and we know that he will not take such a step save in the most exceptional circumstances, where his overall plan for the redemption of the world and the harmonisation of all created beings (including the angels) with his love and his will is imperilled.

The fact that we – that is, all members of the human race – however evil, possess souls having eternal being does not alone suffice to fit us to be members of God's army. We must be able to receive and understand his commands, and this is rendered possible by the fact that every soul is linked to God by a bond, unbreakable by us or by any creature, whether angelic or human. This is the bond or channel of obligation; it is by means of this bond that we are made spiritually aware of the existence of God and of the concepts of obligation and duty. This awareness and these concepts are transferred by our souls to our minds, which may accept or reject them as tenable hypotheses and motivating factors, but cannot deny their existence. The bond of obligation is also a channel through which we learn that the prime duty imposed by our relationship with God is to fight and defeat Satan. It is also the channel through which Christ, if we allow him, gives us his instructions for the conduct of the war. The bond of obligation is also a feature of all angels who, however sinful, have remained loyal to God, but in the case of Satan and his followers has been severed by their expulsion from heaven.

It is important to note that although Satan has access to our souls he cannot break the bond of obligation, nor can he attain direct access to it. What he can do is to try to persuade our souls to block this bond, which is also a channel, so as to deny entry to our souls by the Holy Spirit, which is constantly striving to convey to our souls both God's love and his instructions. If Satan is successful in this, he uses the power which we thus confer on him to pollute our souls and to divert them from their duty.

The biblical phrase used to describe the special relationship with God which we, alone among all his creatures on earth, enjoy is that we are made 'in God's image' (Genesis i, 26, 27). This phrase is apt, for in fact we are able, to a limited extent and if we make the right choices, to absorb some part of God's essence and to reflect it to the world. We can do more, for by creating us in his image God has surrendered to us part of his sovereignty; he has even given us the power, to a limited degree, to compel him to act, or to cease from acting, in a manner other than he would have adopted if we had not interfered. Thus whenever we kill an animal, whether for our food or in self-defence or for sport, or when we kill a plant, we compel God to withdraw his life-sustaining activity by which that animal or plant had been maintained as a living being. (It may be noted that this argument does not apply when one animal kills another, for in so doing the animal is not exercising free will, it is merely acting in accordance with the divinely ordained laws of its being.) On the positive side, whenever a man and a woman unite to create a new human being, they compel God to create a soul to give it a spiritual dimension, conferring on it humanity and personality; in fact transforming it from an 'it' to a 'he' or a 'she'. When we consider this aspect of birth we are, in my view, forced to the conclusion that a soul is created and implanted at the moment of fertilisation. An even more significant example of human power over God, or rather, of God's surrendering some of his power to us, is that by giving us free will he has enabled us to act in opposition to his strategy and his will, thereby compelling him to alter his tactics to accommodate the changing pattern of events of which we have been the cause.

Nothing in this section should be read as implying that we do not have to pass a test. In fact, every soldier in God's army, of whatever rank, whether commissioned or non-commissioned, is being constantly tested as to his or her performance. The most severe tests will be applied to commissioned officers according to rank (that is, to those who aspire to be leaders of thought and to guide the development of humanity, whether in philosophy, moral theory, religion, or politics, or to enhance their understanding of the essence of God as revealed in art); non-commissioned officers and privates have less responsible but equally important and equally valuable tasks and will be tested accordingly. But while the fact that we are all members of an army and that this army is engaged in a war of eternal significance must be constantly kept in mind, we should also note that there is an important distinction to be drawn between God's army and national armies engaged in world wars. This is that, unlike the six hundred of Tennyson's poem 'Their's not to reason why, Their's but to do and die', every member of God's army, from field marshal to private, has equal and immediate access to the Commander-in-Chief, who is Christ. He is approachable at all times and he knows that we shall do what is required of us more efficiently if he shows his confidence in us by revealing as much of his strategy as we can safely be entrusted with. We for our part are under a duty to reciprocate by making full use of Christ's readiness to respond, and particularly when we are engaged in the fiercest strifes. We need not fear that our frailty, our lack of understanding or even our deliberate disobedience to his commands will be any bar to his readiness to respond, or that he will be overwhelmed by too much importunity; being infinite, he is not subject to any limitations. He can deal with an unlimited number of petitions for guidance at the same time, and is always ready to guide and help us in the conduct of the war and in building God's kingdom on earth.

It must, of course, be understood that although knowledge

of one's particular task, as well as courage and resolution on the part of every individual soldier, is vital for the successful conduct of the war, no soldier is fighting for his or her own cause. The conduct of the war must be a co-operative effort, and from this it follows that, while individual petitions will always be heard, those of large groups of people seeking to know what should be their common objective are more vital to the successful conduct of the war, and are likely to be given precedence.

In this section I have tried to show that all the steps taken by God were inevitable. They were logically inherent in God throughout all eternity*, which, being infinite, has no beginning and will have no end, and we can imagine that a fictional being external to God and taking note of his essence could predict the existence of angels, the rebellion of Satan, and the four steps taken by God to remedy the situation brought about by Satan's defection and to give expression to the ultimate objective inherent in his own Being. Thus there is a sense in which we can say that the whole of reality is fore-ordained, but this does not imply that the actions of human beings or their ultimate fate are predestined. In short, the history of the universe, in general though not in detail, flows from the statement that 'God is love'.

---

*It is difficult to avoid using words implying that God dwells in eternity, but this of course is not the case, else eternity would be logically prior to God. God is not only Omega, he is also Alpha; he is prior to eternity, which proceeds from him (page 28). If we must assign a dwelling place for God, we may call it supra-eternity, but in doing so we must recognise that this is no more than another name for God. God and supra-eternity are identical.

3

The Conduct of the War and the Conquest of Death

Summary

In the first two chapters of this book we have been examining the most fundamental question that can be asked about our existence: the question Why are we here? Probably most people, on considering this question, admit its importance, but decide that as it has no obvious answer it is best to ignore it and get on with the difficult business of living, which provides plenty of practical and moral problems to engage all their attention. They might say that they are here to provide food, clothing and shelter for themselves and their families, and care for those to whom they feel that they owe a responsibility. They accept that their efforts to meet these necessities must be governed by rules and that these rules have a wider application, imposing on them duties relating to the well-being of their friends and neighbours, the nation to which they belong, the whole human race and the world into which they have been born. They hope that if they meet the obligations imposed on them by these necessities and duties reasonably satisfactorily, they will have done all that is required of them in their earthly life. Some may, if pressed, admit that in a life after death they may not be able to ignore the fundamental question, but their attitude to this possibility is that they will cross that bridge when they come to it. But although this may be the attitude of the majority of people, there are others who are not satisfied with this dismissive reply; they recognise that the question is of vital importance for the well-being of humankind during earthly life and they look around to see what answers have been proposed. They find that there are at least three.

The first is to deny that the question exists, or that it has any meaning. Those who take this stance argue that we are here as the result of evolution, which does not have any ultimate objective. If we press them, asking why we experience pleasure and pain, they reply that these are necessary to enable natural selection to do its work satisfactorily; and if we go further and ask why we enjoy art and music, their answer is that these emotions are adjuncts to, or developments of, the sexual instinct. If we press them to the limit by asking why we have a moral sense, their answer is that this is in reality no more than a sense of what is expedient and what is inexpedient. We know that if we treat other people badly they may retaliate by treating us badly, so we usually treat them well in the hope that they in return will treat us well. We magnify these instincts of self-protection into the idea of right and wrong merely to flatter our self-importance.

Most people, however, would agree that this answer is unsatisfactory. While admitting that the question exists and demands a positive answer, they feel impelled, because of its difficulty, to thrust it aside, and they find that this can most easily be done by accepting the test theory which we considered in Chapter 1. We are here for the greater glory of God, who has implanted in us the sense of right and wrong. The test theory has the great advantage that it is, when presented in these general terms, very easy to understand. Briefly, it says that if we do what is right we shall be rewarded and if we do what is wrong we shall be punished. Children can grasp this very early, and it appeals to their sense of fairness. Moreover, although neither the Old nor the New Testament gives us full guidance on the moral issues which bewilder us in the overcomplex society we have built up in the twentieth century, Paul gives us in general terms a list of the characteristics which are the gift of the Spirit and which we should aim at cultivating. He also lists the types of behaviour we should avoid. Thus he tells the Galatians that 'Anyone can see the behaviour that belongs to the unspiritual nature; fornication, indecency and debauchery; idolatory and sorcery; quarrels, a contentious temper, envy, fits of rage, selfish ambitions, dissensions, party intrigues, and jealousies; drinking bouts, orgies and the like. I warn you, as I warned you before, that no one who behaves like that will ever inherit the kingdom of God. But the harvest of the Spirit is love, joy, peace, patience, kindness, goodness, fidelity, gentleness, and self-control' (Galatians v, 19–23; see also Ephesians iv, 29–v, 5; 1 Thessalonians v, 13–22).

It is obvious that those who obey these precepts will not go far wrong. But Paul takes no account of the genetic and environmental factors which largely, though by no means entirely, govern our behaviour. The test theory alone is therefore inadequate as an answer to the question why we are here. It cannot be reconciled with the concept of God as a rational Being unless it is supplemented by assigning to him a definable purpose. We are therefore driven to accept, as a reason for our existence, the conclusion reached in the previous section, namely that we have been purposefully created by God to serve as an army for the defeat of Satan, and thereby to pave the way for his redemption.

Since this is the true answer to the question Why are we here? it must be taught to children from their earliest years, and constantly reiterated. This truth must be conveyed to them in such convincing terms that it is never thereafter questioned, but is accepted as a fact as obvious as that the sun will rise and set every day. Admittedly this is not an easy task, for the enemy against whom the war has to be waged is not a physical being; he is invisible but is nevertheless very real. We are not fighting against flesh and blood; our enemies, as Paul says, are principalities and powers, the rulers of the darkness of this world, and wickedness in high places (Ephesians vi, 12).

Another difficult lesson to be learned is that, as members of an army, our responsibility extends beyond coping with the personal problems presented by the situation in which we find ourselves at any time. Each of us has an allotted task to perform in the conduct of the war, a task which is initially imposed at, or shortly after, the time of birth, and is continually renewed and developed as we pass through life. The first task imposed is very light and is discharged in an infant's response to its parents' love; if a child dies in infancy its task will usually be taken over and discharged by its parents, especially by its mother. It is probably discharged, in a way that we cannot fully understand, by their grief, and by the actions of others to which this grief gives rise. In assigning our tasks, God takes note of the faculties we possess by virtue of heredity, and of the manner in which those faculties have been developed or altered by our environment; at any time of our life, therefore, it may be expected that what he wants us to do in the war against Satan and in building his kingdom on earth will be related to the work by which we earn our living or the manner in which we employ our talents in our leisure time, though this is not necessarily the case. The variety of gifts enabling us to perform our tasks is listed by Paul in his letter to the Romans (chapter xii, 5–8) and his first letter to the Corinthians (chapter xii, 7–12). If he were writing today, he might have added the gifts of controlling the dominance of economics and of retarding the onward march of technology. In both these passages Paul emphasises that in Christ we are all members of one body, and from this it follows that the performance of each individual task must be seen as part of a global strategy.

In personal terms, the manner in which the task confronting me at any time is performed, whether it is performed well or badly, or is shunted off, is of concern not only to me, but to everyone in the world. For an army is not a collection of individual soldiers, it is a team with a common objective. If I shirk my duty, Satan gains an advantage which he will use when and where it suits him best. My failure may result in an additional burden being placed on someone, or on a group of people, who may live in my neighbourhood or at the other end of the world. On the positive side, every victory over Satan will benefit not only the person who is responsible for it but may have beneficial repercussions over a wide area. As in an earthly war, both these features of the war with Satan are particularly marked when a victory is gained, or a defeat suffered, by a group of people co-operating in a common effort.

The fact that every individual has been assigned one or more specific tasks in the working out of God's purpose (Ephesians i, 11) reveals the true meaning of predestination. Predestination does not mean that every soul, at the moment of its creation, is predestined to ultimate salvation or damnation, although some verses of scripture might be read as having this meaning (e.g. Romans viii, 28–30). Nor does it mean that God has foreknowledge, when he creates a soul to be the guiding light of a newborn child or a foetus, of whether that soul will discharge its task to his satisfaction. Such interpretations are wholly incompatible with the fact that every soul is free and that God is a loving Father to all humankind. Predestination does, however, mean more than that every individual has his or her part to play in God's plan; it applies also in a special way to all those who follow a particular vocation, profession or other occupation, and especially to all artists, all writers, all philosophers, all theologians and religious teachers (of all religions, including non-theistic religions such as Buddhism and humanism) and other leaders of thought. Thus every person has his or her predestined tasks stemming from different sources, as an individual, as a worker by hand or brain, as a follower of a particular religion, as a member of a tribe or nation with its own particular culture and constitution. It is perhaps necessary to say that Satan will do his utmost to ensure that the duties imposed by the various categories into which every person has to fit himself shall conflict, so as to render the performance of those duties as difficult as possible.

Another very important lesson is that the true objective of the human race – the defeat of Satan – must be incorporated into the teaching of history. The meaning of history will not be learned by acquiring knowledge of past events, even if these are woven into a larger pattern, e.g. the advance of forms of government, the rise and fall of empires, the conflict between church and state, or any other broad idea. The student of history (and to some extent this should include everyone) must learn how the facts of history illustrate the effort to achieve the true goal of humanity and to what extent they have promoted or retarded the achievement of that goal. As Josef Pieper has said: 'In history, it is not the past, not "what actually happened" which is of philosophic interest... What really and in the deepest analysis happens in history is salvation and disaster.'* In this passage 'salvation' does not mean personal salvation, it means the salvation of the human race. In the teaching of history, the defeat of Satan, the building of God's kingdom and the salvation of humankind must be seen as three different descriptions of the same enterprise and as the end towards which all human effort must be directed.

These are hard lessons, and anyone who is told that they cannot be evaded because they define the meaning of life on earth is likely to say, 'I am not a soldier; I am a lover of peace; if I am to be press-ganged into an army against my will, what profit is there in it for me at the end?' There are two answers to this. The first is that given by the test theory, which, as we have seen (pages 16–17) is not false, but is incomplete as a description of God's purpose. The ultimate reward for the successful conduct of the war will be the gift of eternal life but, since all have sinned (Romans iii, 23), all will from time to time have failed to some extent in their duties and will have to undergo further training, or even punishment, before being admitted to eternal life. The punishment, however, will be no greater than is necessary to bring the sinner to acknowledge his failings and to repent.

The second answer is that God has rendered our task easier by linking the defeat of Satan with the building of his kingdom on earth. These two aspects of our task cannot be separated. Every success in the conduct of war, whether by an individual or by the community, advances the building of God's kingdom, and every setback either delays it or destroys some part of what has been built. Likewise, every step taken towards building God's kingdom on earth, every thought or act inspired by the presence of Christ in the soul, and every

---

The End of Time, Faber and Faber, 1954, pp. 13 and 22.

temptation resisted, again whether by an individual or by the community at large, either inflicts a wound on Satan or causes him to abandon ground which he had earlier occupied and in which he had believed that he was secure. If (as we must) we believe that God is good then everyone will admit that building his kingdom on earth is a worthwhile occupation, and the task of teaching both children and adults that they must engage in the war against Satan is rendered relatively easy.

Thus although the purpose for which we have been created would appear to have two distinct elements, these are, and will ultimately be seen to be, identical. While we still see them as distinct we must try to give them equal importance. If we lay too much emphasis on the military aspect of our duty we may lose heart, as Satan will always find means of attacking us on new fronts. This error is also likely to lead to a distorted ethic, in which too much emphasis is laid on the domination of one group by another and on obedience to orders. If, on the other hand, we dismiss the idea of Satan as an enemy to be defeated and concentrate on building the kingdom of God, the consequences will be that, without our being aware of it, Satan will mislead us and we shall find that the kingdom we are building has been largely designed by him. If we ignore Satan we are likely also to forget to submit ourselves to God. We shall try to build the kingdom of God without reference to him whose realm it is, relying on our own judgment as to what the kingdom, when built, will be like, and our judgment will be faulty, because Satan will lose no opportunity to pervert it. Only God knows fully the conditions that will prevail in his kingdom on earth, and these may prove to be very different from what we, in our immature state of development, may consider to be utopian. This error, therefore, is also likely to lead to a distorted ethic, in which individuality, liberty and equality are given undue prominence. It is an error into which we have been particularly liable to fall during the present century. In order to avoid both these faults of emphasis, we must remember that our duties have been imposed by God and that we must continually seek his guidance in discharging them, knowing that his help will be freely given at all times if it is sincerely sought.

It is inevitable that we should ask whether we human beings on earth are alone in the stupendous task of defeating an army of immeasurable size, every soldier in which is endowed with all the powers of the angels. We do not at present know the answer to this question, although it may be revealed to us in due course, and in the meantime we may reasonably hope that we are not without allies. The magnitude of the task of defeating such a formidable enemy must inspire awe, but when we contemplate the immensity of the physical universe and the immeasurably complex variety of the manifestations of the world of mind, we cannot but feel convinced that we are not the only beings on whom God has conferred the faculties to enjoy all these wonders, or endowed with powers and the freedom to choose how to use them. It is therefore very highly probable that there are 'people' in other parts of the universe who have been entrusted with the task of bringing Satan to repentance and redemption. Such people may resemble us only in the fact that they have souls dwelling in eternity and can therefore respond to God's love and receive his instructions, and are free to obey or to disobey them, but who differ from us physically and mentally.

If this hypothesis is true, then it is also probable that our antagonist is not Satan himself but one of his lieutenants, and that the same applies to each of God's armies in the universe. In that case, it is probably also true that the final assault on Satan will not take place until all his agents have been defeated, and all God's soldiers, the army in which we are one battalion, have completed their tasks, which include not only the defeat of the enemy whom Satan has instructed to attack them, but have gone beyond that and have built the kingdom of God in their dwelling place as far as their inescapable imperfections allow. We are, however, concerned with our own particular enemy, and I shall continue to refer to him as 'Satan', as he is the supreme commander of all his armies, and we do not know the name of the officer designated to attack the earth. It is indeed probable that, in order to create the greatest possible confusion, Satan from time to time replaces the chief officer assigned to each of the planets or other regions engaged in the war. The most senior officer against whom we on earth are at present opposed may well be named 'Mammon'.

It is interesting to note that, when the possibility of the existence of the extraterrestrial people is discussed, the only question raised is whether they are intelligent or how far their intelligence exceeds ours. This is typical of our secular outlook. Intelligence is of course important, but on earth it is not the feature by which human beings are distinguished from other animals, many of which possess limited powers of intelligence. The distinguishing feature of human beings is their possession of a soul having eternal being and therefore free, and from the point of view of the fulfilment of God's plan the same criterion must be applied to extraterrestrial beings. It may be added that while some means of spiritual communication may in due course be established, if God deems that the war with Satan may thereby be more effectively waged, the possibility that such alien beings will ever be able to visit us physically or even communicate with us mentally is so remote that we would be wise to rule it out altogether.

One final point may be made. This is that a moment in time may ultimately come, many thousands of years ahead, when Satan and all his generals and lieutenants, and all his other followers, will admit defeat and will surrender to God. There will then be rejoicing in heaven that the greatest sinner has repented and has been redeemed, but many other angels, whose response to God's love has been negative, will remain disaffected, and further work, in which we shall play a prominent part, will be necessary for their redemption. It is possible that we, and our allies elsewhere in the universe, will not at first know of Satan's surrender, for the work of building God's kingdom will not be complete. This work can in fact never be finished, because God's kingdom is perfect, and we can never achieve perfection, although we can approach it asymptotically. What we shall observe after the defeat of Satan will be that our growth in righteousness will be accelerated, being no longer impeded from outside by Satan but only by the sinfulness from which all created beings must suffer, and that this growth will continue in time for as long as God considers necessary to equip us for such further work in eternity as he may require us to perform.

Weapons and Armoury

The first and most important step to be taken in the conduct of a war is to assess the nature and the power of the weapons available to each combatant. Each side must also seek to discover how his opponent's mind works, so as to be able to forestall his strategy and tactics. We are familiar with the weapons available to Satan, although we cannot always foresee how he will use them and he is adept at concealing their use. These weapons are his power to injure our bodies and to tempt us to break God's commandments, and his skill in perverting our judgment. The devices he adopts to achieve these ends will be considered later.

On the human side, the war must be conducted with the armoury which God has provided for us, and we must believe that, however inadequate it may appear to us, it is, if properly used, the most effective armoury for the purpose that God requires us to fulfil. This armoury consists of our souls, our minds and our bodies. Of these, by far the most important are our souls. Our bodies and minds, although involved, do not decide the main issues. Our minds do indeed make decisions on day-to-day matters concerned with the conduct of the war, but all major decisions are reached by our souls and, more particularly, by the communal soul of a large number of people sharing a common culture. The importance of the communal soul must not be underestimated or undervalued, for souls communicate with one another, not only through the agency of the bodily and mental dwellings in which they are housed. They do, of course, use these agencies in gesture, speech, writing, art and other means of communication, but they also interact directly through a spiritual medium which we cannot describe or define. This interaction is, however, of the very first importance, for when a communal spiritual decision is reached it can determine the direction in which the human race will evolve for several centuries ahead, and the characteristics and faculties that will be developed during that time, to ensure that the decision is made effective.

Thus equipped, our task is to engage, as an army, in the war with Satan. The war has already lasted thousands, possibly hundreds of thousands, of years, and it must be admitted that hitherto our efforts to defeat Satan have not been very successful. Although we have gained some ground, victory is still a distant goal; how distant we do not know, but from our previous experience and from our knowledge of what has yet to be achieved we must expect that the war will continue for many more thousands of years. For in waging the war against Satan we shall at the same time be building the kingdom of God on earth, and we have only to look on the condition of the world around us to be convinced that the task still confronting us is very formidable.

Armies engaging in earthly wars need to be trained, and when possible the necessary training is given before the soldiers are sent into battle. But God has ordained that in the war against Satan his soldiers can best be trained by learning from their mistakes. It often happens that at the time when we commit these mistakes we do not recognise them as such, but later we learn, only to fall into other errors. If we pursue a false objective the consequences will be harmful, and although they may be slow in coming to fruition they are certain. This is a lesson which we must try to absorb throughout the whole of our life, but most particularly during our years of adolescence. It must, however, be learned correctly. Adolescents are not slow to condemn the mistakes which, as it seems to them, have been made by their parents' generation, but their judgment is often superficial, dwelling on social or political errors, whereas the true mistakes lie at a much deeper level. They also tend to ignore the fact that they will in due course have to suffer similar criticism from the next generation.

At first sight it might appear that in the matter of weaponry all the advantages lie with Satan. The most obvious of these advantages is that he is a wholly eternal being. Though expelled from heaven, he remains an angel (and this is also true of all his followers who were cast out with him). He is not encumbered with a body and mind having temporal being, which are weak, liable to disease and ultimately, in earthly terms, mortal, as we are while still on earth. We must, however, firmly resist the idea that this confers an advantage on Satan. God foresaw all the difficulties to which we would be exposed by having bodies and minds as well as souls, but nevertheless so arranged the structure of the universe that we, the soldiers in his army, should be thus equipped. We may be sure that he had good reason for this and we must have faith that he knows best. We know also that our life, though still temporal, continues after earthly death, when our natural bodies and minds are transformed into spiritual bodies and minds having eternal being (1 Corinthians xv, 44). Those who have passed through the gateway of earthly death, therefore, are on an equal footing, ontologically, with Satan, and will be able to fight him with different weapons.

Another circumstance that would appear to be to Satan's advantage is that he has prior knowledge of our situation, whereas we have to learn by experience how and where he will launch his attacks and, as already mentioned, we are often mistaken. He knows that God has created us for the specific purpose of waging war on him and inflicting on him an irreversible defeat so that he is brought to repentance and redemption. He has kept careful watch on our evolution since we first appeared on earth; he understands fully the workings and weaknesses of our bodies and minds, and he has access to our souls, since his mode of being and that of our souls are identical. We, on the other hand, cannot see or hear him and have no sensory knowledge of his existence. Satan, of course, takes advantage of this; one of his most effective ploys is to persuade us that he does not exist. It is probable that if a poll were to be taken, a very large percentage of the population would deny that Satan exists as a real person. They would, of course, admit the existence of evil; they could hardly do otherwise when they look at the conditions prevailing in the world today, but they would say that the evil has its dwelling in the hearts of human beings themselves and is not the defining characteristic of an external person, real though invisible. The danger lying in this false ethic is that it is apt to lead to the conclusion that the world, and in particular human nature, is intrinsically evil, and this belief is liable to degenerate into the belief that the body and its desires are also evil. Even Paul, who, as we know from Ephesians vi, was well aware of the existence of Satan and his followers, in many places opposed 'the flesh' (*sarx*) to 'the spirit', implying that our bodies are intrinsically evil, a belief that directly contradicts Genesis i, 31 and 1 Timothy iv, 4. Peter (or the author of the epistles attributed to him) certainly believed in the existence of Satan; he advises young people to be sober and vigilant, 'because your adversary the devil, as a roaring lion, walketh about, seeking whom he may devour; whom resist steadfast in the faith' (1 Peter v, 8, 9).

The Gnostics confused the issue still further; they admitted the existence of Satan and of the evil desires of 'the flesh'; and accounted for the existing circumstances by maintaining that evil was personified in a god, a lesser god than the true God and perhaps possibly a descendant from him – they constructed elaborate genealogical tables to account for this, and it is notable that Paul warns Timothy against being taken in by these, see 1 Timothy, i, 4. They maintained also that this lesser god created the material universe and is at war with the true God who created the spiritual world. They believed that in this war the human soul is a battleground, not a participant in the fight. These ideas, in one form or another, are still rife today, although they have always been rightly condemned by the Christian churches.

Then again, as we are unable to attack Satan's body, because he does not have one; and having no access to his soul, to implant good objectives, as he can implant evil objectives in our souls, our war with Satan is very largely defensive, an endeavour to repulse his attacks, whereas he has the advantage of surprise, ambush and attack. We can only fight openly and defensively. This, however, is not a real disadvantage because, as we have already seen (pages 62-3), in this war a successful defence is equivalent to an attack. Every act of submission or obedience to God impairs our enemy's power to attack us.

Nevertheless, the advantages held by Satan may seem to be, and indeed are, formidable, but they cannot prevail against the ultimate defensive weapon available to us, if we are willing and ready to use it. This is that we, through the channel of obligation, have direct access to God, a privilege denied absolutely to Satan. Through this channel God conveys his instructions and implants in our souls and minds the concept of duty. If we keep it open, allowing the Holy Spirit to cleanse it of all obstacles, Christ will flow through it into our souls and every attack by Satan will be repulsed. The initiative must be taken by us, but we know that if we seize it, God will respond, for we have the assurance that Christ stands at the door and knocks; if we hear his voice and open the door, he will come in, and we shall sup together (Revelation iii, 20). It is therefore in our interest to keep this channel clear of all obstacles. If it becomes obstructed or polluted, as it will be not only by sin, but also by wrongful desires and false beliefs, it must be cleansed, but we must not expect the Holy Spirit to cleanse our link with God unless we ask him, and our petition must be sincere, wholehearted and unqualified.

In all cases in which we seek the help of the Father, the Son or the Holy Spirit our request must be accompanied by a genuine effort on our part to achieve the desired end. It is by the measure of our effort that the sincerity of our petition will be judged and a response given. We are therefore driven to ask what we must do to satisfy God that our request for the cleansing power of the Holy Spirit is genuine. To this question the obvious answer is that, since God is love (agape), we must ensure that all our thoughts, all our words and all our actions are inspired and guided by agapeic love. We are indeed instructed that it is our duty, second only to loving God (Deuteronomy vi, 4, 5; Mark xii, 29, 30), to love (*agapein*) our neighbour as ourself (Leviticus xix, 18; Mark xii, 31). This is therefore a divinely given rule, and we must not only mould our characters but also direct our evolution (see page 73) in such a way as to create conditions in which it can be consistently obeyed. But in present conditions this is not possible. It is true that in very simple personal relations the rule may be an adequate guide, but even in these cases, if the problem to be addressed is complex or is one extending over a period of time (e.g. to what extent should example be supplemented by discipline in the upbringing of children), it is often found to be inadequate because of the difficulty of interpreting it in action. When we come to consider more complex problems, such as the behaviour of large-scale organisations, the framing of legislation or the administration of justice, it is a very poor guide, because there are so many competing interests that in showing agape towards one we may be showing enmity towards, or at least damaging, others.

We therefore need further guidance in our effort to understand the meaning of agape and to learn how it should govern our actions and decisions in the complex circumstances with which we are daily confronted. In this difficult task, which is also the task of maintaining and strengthening the link with God which is the key to our victory over Satan, we need God's help, and this can only be obtained by prayer. This does not mean that we must be constantly on our knees asking forgiveness for our sins or petitioning God for some benefit we hope to receive from him, though both of these, particularly the first, are necessary from time to time. It means integrating our concept of agape with recognition of the purpose for which we were created. To be more specific, it means keeping unceasingly in mind the facts: (1) that we are on a crusade to build God's kingdom – the new Jerusalem (Revelation xxi, 2) – on earth; (2) that although we have a general idea of the direction of the new Jerusalem the road is very rough and much of it has to be constructed as we go along; (3) that Satan is our enemy and will use every possible device to impede us and to divert us into false paths; (4) that we will not know, if we rely on our unaided judgment, that we are being misled; (5) that God will guide us aright if we allow him to do so; and (6) that on reaching our goal we shall receive both personal salvation and the salvation of humankind, but that, while we are still on the crusade, the latter must always have priority in our minds. And finally, we must recognise that the complexities which cloud our judgment are largely of our own making and must be controlled and lessened as we build God's kingdom. It is only then that we can create the conditions in which agape can rule our lives.

Thus armed, we have the enormous advantage of knowing that we can win the war. We can even be more positive, for God has ensured, by sending his Son to dwell among us, that we *will* win the war; if, therefore, our faith remains undimmed we may know that our success is certain. For God will not allow the struggle to have an outcome in which the sacrifice offered by his Son has been made in vain. Satan has not this advantage; he hopes to win, but he cannot know that he will win. We must therefore keep these truths unceasingly in the background of our minds, and from time to time we should bring them into the foreground, especially when we are faced with some difficult decision, so that we are consciously aware that we are allowing Christ to be our guide.

Satan, being an angel, albeit a fallen angel, has eternal being, but this does not in itself confer on him any advantage over us, as our souls also have eternal being. We have, however, seen that eternal beings are free, and from this we can infer that they can perform miracles; in other words, they can be the cause of an event or a sequence of events in the natural world of time and space which would not have occurred, or would have occurred in a different way, if the physical, psychical and interactive laws operative in that world had not been interfered with by the eternal being. This inference can be made because if the eternal realm, in its contact with the natural world, were compelled to allow that world to be governed by its own laws without interference, its freedom would be null and void. This power of working miracles does give Satan, temporarily, some advantage over us, for although our souls and wills are free from *constraint* by God (i.e. he does not compel them to act in a particular way), and they also can perform miracles, they are to some extent subject to *restraint* by him (i.e. he does not allow them to exercise all their latent powers to the full, lest in our immature state we should misuse them). Satan, on the other hand, is subject neither to constraint nor restraint. This advantage, however, will gradually be eliminated, for as we build God's kingdom on earth and become more mature, the restraints imposed by God will gradually be lifted.

The soul of every human being, when first created, is a *tabula rasa*, a clean slate on which to write its own agenda. It is free to select its own objectives, and the only earthly source from which it can make its selection is the growing content of the mind, as the developing mind of the child, and later of the adult, gains knowledge of the world on which it has been placed. In particular, the soul takes note of the natural desires for food, drink, sex, shelter and freedom from danger which are essential elements in the mind of all living creatures and have been developed by the operation of the laws of evolution. It also takes note of the faculties available to it and of the desires that heredity and environment have engendered and of any other personality characteristics of the body and mind of its host, i.e. of the person in whom it is lodged.

It should, however, be noted that, as a consequence of the distinction between the modes of being possessed by our souls and our minds, the traffic between them is one-way (see pages 38–39). Our minds cannot compel our souls to choose any particular objective, but they can lay before them a range of objectives from which our souls can make a selection. Our souls, having done this, can create, modify or annul desires, beliefs and faculties in such a way as to further the achievement of their chosen objectives. In this way the soul of every individual can mould his or her character, overriding (to some extent) the influences of heredity and environment. Even more significantly, the souls of a group of people sharing a common culture and a common objective can, by inducing mutations, mould the evolution of that group over several generations to ensure that that objective is achieved. In those activities they can, if they so choose, seek the guidance of God, with whom they are connected by the bond of obligation. Too often, however, they either misread this guidance or ignore it.

Satan's Tactics

Satan, knowing that we are a trinity of soul, mind and body, attacks all three aspects of our personalities, although in different ways. He cannot exercise his thaumaturgic powers on our souls, since their mode of being is the same as his, but he uses those powers unceasingly on our minds and bodies. His attack on our souls takes the form of persuasion; knowing that the soul, when not guided by God, selects its long-term objectives from those presented to it by the mind, he concentrates his efforts on persuading the soul to adopt those objectives that will most effectively block the channel of obligation. In the case of individuals, he makes use of the natural inclinations derived from their heredity and environment, concentrating particularly on such characteristics as the love of power or money. His main attack, however, is on the souls of a group of people having a common culture, persuading them to adopt objectives which, perhaps over several generations, will lead to social and economic conditions that will seriously impede the building of God's kingdom.

As regards our bodies, Satan knows that, although they are frail, it is God's will that they should be healthy. This is perhaps obvious, but if verification is needed we have Paul's assurance that the body is the temple of the Holy Spirit (1 Corinthians vi, 19); it is also proved by the fact that Christ spent much of his time while on earth in healing the sick. Satan can here use his power to perform miracles (pages 72–3); but in the nature of things, we cannot easily distinguish between those bodily ailments that should be attributed to him from those having a natural cause. It is possible that one of his activities is to induce a pattern of life that will ensure that many children are born with some physical disability, such as malformation of the limbs, Down's syndrome or autism. We certainly cannot rule out the possibility that he played a significant part in the thalidomide disaster. Another possibility is that he can create genetic modifications in pathogenic organisms so as to render them more virulent, and it is probable that he is active in spreading the Aids virus.

We have the evidence of Jesus himself to support the belief that Satan has the power to injure our bodies, for it is recorded that he attributed the disability of a crippled woman to him (Luke xiii, 16). We do not know how effectively Satan uses his power to achieve his ends, but it is certain that he directs some of his energy to distorting the natural desires for food, drink and sex, which God has implanted in us to maintain our species in being and in fit condition to conduct the war. In this, however, Satan has not been wholly successful. The majority of people are reasonably abstemious, holding, with Juvenal, that it is desirable, indeed that it should be a petition in our prayers, to have a healthy mind in a healthy body. Nevertheless, the evils that spring from excess seem to become more horrific every day, as we read of the violence induced by drink, leading to separation or divorce, or even to murder, and of the sexual assaults, often followed by murder, on children by men unable to control their lust. We can see that the Roman Catholics have been wise to include gluttony and lust among the seven deadly sins. Recently, however, Satan has not confined his activity to exploiting the body's natural desires; he has aimed at disabling the bodies of his enemies, God's soldiers, by introducing them to addictive drugs and by multiplying the number and variety of such drugs, thereby creating unnatural and very powerful desires which are self-reproducing. In this evil activity he has taken as his target the most vulnerable members of society, and has induced them to create a culture in which the abuse of their bodies in this way is regarded as good. He therefore has the satisfaction of damaging their consciences as well as their bodies.

The mind is the gateway to the soul and is constantly interacting with the body. It is not surprising, therefore, that Satan concentrates his main effort on perverting, depraving and corrupting our minds. There he finds – in the immense variety of experiences our minds enjoy, in the faculties they can use to pursue their chosen ends, and the ends chosen by the souls to which they are linked – fertile ground and ample scope for his activities, and he makes full use of the opportunities thus provided.

It would be impossible to list all the devices he employs to achieve his ends, not only because of their number and variety, but also because he is constantly altering them to take account of changing circumstances. We can, however, identify some of these devices and also some basic characteristics of all his attacks.

First, knowing that God has implanted in us the power to know something of his essence through the medium of art, Satan tries unceasingly to pervert our sense of artistic appreciation. He does this in two ways – first by implanting in our minds the idea that the object of all art is not the revelation of God's essence but something other and therefore lower, e.g. the portrayal of the world as it really is, or as the artist would like to persuade us that it really is; and secondly by allowing us to retain the true object of art, while he masquerades as God (2 Corinthians xi, 14), so that the work produced, claiming to be true art, is in fact a revelation of his own Satanic nature.

There can be no doubt that in both of these means of perverting our judgment and in alienating us from God he has had remarkable success during the present century. There have, of course, been some artistic productions that truly reveal God's essence, in so far as it has lain in the artists' understanding and technical ability to do this, and to the artists who have provided this revelation we must show both respect and gratitude; but there have also been too many productions claiming to be artistic that have been largely inspired by Satan. Some of these have done real damage to our minds and, if our souls have allowed themselves to be misled, to them also. Others have been merely silly, although many critics, fearful of being dubbed reactionary and opposed to avant-garde culture, have tried to persuade us otherwise. It is possible that the perpetrators of these insubstantial productions have intended no harm, but have set out to discover or to reveal how gullible the public, deprived of true guidance by those whose duty it is to provide such guidance, can be. Very often the popularity of a 'work of art' of this genre, or the vogue for a style falling in this category, is short-lived, so that little harm is done, and God in his mercy may decide to overlook such childish pranks;

but this does not alter the fact that what the so-called artist has done is wrong, because it is a breach of the third Commandment – thou shalt not take the name of the Lord thy God in vain. But even if these productions do little damage they certainly give comfort to Satan, and on the assumption that he has a sense of humour we may believe that he finds them hugely entertaining. This assumption is reasonable, because we know that he can pervert our sense of humour by persuading some foolish people to play practical jokes which do real damage to their victims.

Another example of the debasement of art during the twentieth century is provided by architecture; the origin and influence of much that has been produced during the past fifty or sixty years has been the glorification of Mammon rather than of God. This is certainly true of commercial architecture, but it also applies to domestic architecture, as exemplified by the high-rise blocks of flats that were erected in the 1960s and 1970s. It is probable, however, that more than one agent of Satan was involved in inspiring the building of these monstrosities; in order to inflict the maximum damage on those who are compelled to live in them, Mammon enlisted the aid of other devils, including possibly Moloch. It is to our credit that we are now demolishing some of these generators of crime and vandalism and replacing them by dwellings of a size and design more suitable for the growth of the souls of those who live in them and for the development of personal relations with their neighbours.

Satan has also been active in trying to debase music. In this field, however, it is difficult to judge how far he has succeeded. Serious music has become so complex and in some cases so discordant that time will be needed to assess its effect on our minds and souls. It would seem, however, that in our judgment of the value of music we are more selective than in the case of other arts. To listen to a symphony or concerto lasting three-quarters of an hour requires more mental effort and concentration than to look at a painting or a sculpture (though these also require careful and even prolonged study) and we easily reject what we find to be too exhausting. What can be said with certainty is that Satan has concentrated his efforts on the easier target of 'pop' music. Here he has found it possible to attack our bodies indirectly by persuading us that it must be played so loudly as to damage our ears, and with the accompaniment of stroboscopic lighting that damages our eyes. Here also he has selected as his main target the most vulnerable members of society and has compounded the evil by linking some of the more extreme varieties of this music with violence (gangsta-rap) and drugs (rave).

We are all prone to misunderstand theological truths, which deal with statements and facts relating to the eternal order, and these cannot be verified or falsified by any of the scientific or other methods applicable to statements about the world in which we live. We can, therefore, easily misunderstand the statement that the purpose of art is to glorify God and to reveal his essence. This might be read as meaning that true art is limited to the building of cathedrals and churches, the portrayal of religious subjects and the composition and performance of sacred music. It might also be taken to mean that no atheist can be a true artist. Neither of these limiting interpretations, however, would be correct. An artist may declare himself to be an atheist, but this is an intellectual statement and may not represent the true state of his soul, which may have kept its link with God uncluttered. For the soul and the intellect may be in conflict; the declaration of a belief may have no firmer basis than a desire to conform to the current philosophy of the group to which the artist belongs. Harmony between the soul and the mind is obviously more likely to beget great art than conflict, but the latter is not an insuperable barrier.

Moreover, the essence of God can be revealed and God can be glorified in a secular context. This fact is obviously true, because the physical and mental worlds are part of God's creation. A true work of art may even depict human beings in circumstances brought about by their frailty or by the knowledge of their mortality, provided that the work gives encouragement or comfort to those whose souls are, consciously or unconsciously, trying to build God's kingdom. It would be unwise to be too prescriptive, but it is probable that no work which depicts human beings as mere mechanical devices, incapable of experiencing or expressing faith, hope or charity, can be a true work of art. Perhaps the most obvious example of art that contains no religious element is pure mathematics. It is also the only art that Satan finds it impossible to penetrate.

Although the potential evil wrought by Satan's attack on our aesthetic sense, leading to a false evaluation of artistic merit, must not be underrated, and although both those who produce artistic works and those who simply enjoy them must strive to bring this sense into alignment with God's will, Satan recognises that true art has a power of endurance that he cannot destroy, and that his main attack on this front can achieve little more than the corruption of fashions in minor arts, which are often ephemeral. His main effort is therefore directed to perverting our desires and beliefs, and through our beliefs, our consciences. His power to direct these to his own ends is almost unlimited.

One of Satan's most effective weapons in his war against us is the implantation and fostering of the desire to dominate. This desire is, of course, directly opposed to the statement made by Christ: 'Blessed are the meek, for they shall inherit the earth' (Matthew v, 5), but Satan has no difficulty in countering this. He induces us to create conditions in which Christ's words are not denied absolutely, but are regarded as impossibly utopian. In this he has had remarkable success. But since he knows that we attach weight to the Beatitudes he persuades us to believe that, although the necessary ideal conditions can never be reached, they can be approached if we follow his lead.

Having done this, he encourages us to transform the necessary element of competition in our personalities, which is part of God's plan (see pages 14-15), into the desire to compel others to conform to our wishes or, less excusably, to humiliate them. This desire to dominate leads to bullying in school and office; it often leads to the breakdown of marriages, and it shows itself in its most potent and evil form in the establishment of tyrannical dictatorships which are so prominent in the world today. Finally, it can degenerate into the ultimate evil of desiring to inflict cruelty on those within our power, and of taking pleasure in doing so. This desire probably has its origin in fear, an instinctual reaction to threatening circumstances, which God has implanted in us to ensure our survival. It can also be triggered by a desire for revenge against someone who we think has injured us, or has aroused a very strong feeling of disapproval by some outrageous act, such as an act of cruelty to a child or other defenceless person. Satan has, of course, seized on the instinct of fear and has corrupted it into the desire to inflict cruelty, and it is a salutory thought that this desire is held by everyone (except possibly by a few saints), though probably in a mild form, expressing itself in anger or abuse. It should be noted that we are specifically warned against harbouring feelings of revenge; this feature of retribution is reserved to God alone (Deuteronomy xxxii, 35; Romans xii, 19). We are, of course, permitted to punish wrongdoers, but if we allow the administration of justice to be contaminated by the desire for revenge we are damaging our own souls.

Satan's power to attack us through our desires is formidable and difficult to resist, but God, recognising this, has given us a positive weapon to reinforce the negative weapon of resistance. This is the desire, prompted by conscience, to act in accordance with what we believe to be right. This desire, though linked with conscience, is distinct from it, and it is important that the two should not be confused. As we have seen (page 39), conscience is a spiritual faculty, an element present in our souls, flowing into them through the channel of obligation, whereby we acquire and are capable of understanding the concept of duty towards God. Unlike a duty to an earthly authority, however, which is imposed and enforced by that authority, our duty to God is not imposed; it is simply lodged in the soul and is transmitted by the soul to the mind, which translates it into the concepts of right and wrong, and also decides *what* is right and *what* is wrong. In doing this the mind draws its inspiration partly through the soul from God and partly from earthly sources. Conscience is not itself a desire, but may be regarded as the parent of the desire to conform to a normative code. This desire, however, like all offspring, develops its own characteristics, and the code to which it gives loyalty may differ from that dictated by conscience. In part this code may be self-generated, but the greater part of it is governed by what is considered right and honourable by the group to which one belongs, and the desire is associated with the universal desire to stand well in the sight of those with whom we are most closely associated. It can, however, go a long way beyond this and may be the cause of great acts of heroism or self-sacrifice, even in cases where those who perform them know that they will never become known to the outside world.

Although Satan's attempts to corrupt our desires can be very harmful, and if not resisted will certainly delay the coming of God's kingdom, he finds that the most effective means of causing lasting damage is to implant in our minds false beliefs. By this means he can, without our being aware of it, impede us in the performance of our duty and, even more harmfully, mislead us as to where our duty lies. In this connection it may be noted that desires do not often influence beliefs (except in the trivial case of 'wishful thinking'), but beliefs can give birth to a desire (or a complex of desires) that will, if satisfied, render that belief factual. This is most notable where a belief is held by a large number of people in communication with one another. The belief will then be taken over by the communal soul, which will foster the appropriate desires and create the faculties whereby those desires can be satisfied.

Satan's attack on our beliefs is therefore fundamental and all-important. Two false beliefs have already been mentioned: the belief that he does not exist (pages 68–9) and the belief that the ideas and desires implanted by him are really divine revelations (pages 16 and 76). These, however, are ancillary beliefs, which he uses to supplement and reinforce the positive false beliefs on which he relies to frustrate our efforts to build the kingdom of God.

These positive beliefs are usually presented to us in such a form as to convince us that by accepting them we are obeying

God's commandment to love our neighbour. Satan achieves this by ensuring that, though basically false and certainly very damaging if adopted uncritically, they often contain a measure of truth. This gives him an immensely powerful weapon; he stresses the benefits to humankind that will flow from adopting the belief and putting it into practice, and does his best to conceal all its evil consequences.

Satan, of course, varies his assaults on our beliefs to suit the circumstances prevailing at the time. This, however, does not always mean that an old belief is annulled and replaced by new beliefs. A false belief implanted in the communal mind may be very tenacious of life, and if adopted by the communal soul as an objective may persist for several centuries, although with changing circumstances it may be expressed in a different form, possibly less openly in words and less spectacularly in action than when first adopted. It may, on the other hand, develop into a kindred but equally false belief, involving new forms of expression that are at least as evil as those attaching to the original belief. Examples of this persistence will be readily seen in some of the false beliefs described in the following paragraphs.

At an early stage in the rise of Christianity Satan implanted the belief that personal salvation could only be achieved by strict adherence to all the doctrines laid down by the church. This requirement would be valid if the time allowed for compliance includes life after as well as before death, and if the doctrines to which assent is demanded are limited to those laid down by the early Church Councils, for it seems certain that those councils were guided by the Holy Spirit. It is certainly not valid if 'doctrine' is held to include every pronouncement made by every Pope or every statement contained in the Thirty-Nine Articles of the Anglican Church. This false belief was at one time linked to the belief that it is the duty of the church to compel everyone to proclaim his or her acceptance of the church's doctrines while still alive on earth; and it led, quite illogically, to the decision to terminate the lives of those who refused to make this proclamation by burning them at the stake, instead of doing everything possible to prolong their lives in the hope that they might be persuaded to accept the church's teaching. Thus the initial false belief led to the barbarity of the Inquisition and, in England, to the execution, by burning or otherwise, of Protestants in the reign of Mary and of Roman Catholics in the reign of Elizabeth I. It also led to the iniquitous imbecility of Oliver Cromwell to order the destruction of images and other works of art in our cathedrals and churches.

The belief that adherence to true doctrine is necessary for salvation is a valid belief, but it becomes perverted when we assume that we are sufficiently enlightened to know with certainty which doctrines are true and which are false. The facts that there are so many religions in the world, and that in many of these (particularly in Christianity) there are different sects more or less openly quarrelling with one another (as in Northern Ireland), ought to convince us that this assumption is false; but Satan delights in persuading the adherents of every sectarian creed that, while others may be partially justified in their beliefs, they alone are in possession of the whole truth and are therefore entitled to treat those who disagree with them as enemies of the truth: and therefore of God.

Closely allied to the belief that the revelation of true doctrine is the prerogative of a particular sect is the even more evil belief that one group of people, or one tribe, or one race is responsible for all the evil in the world. This belief, though perhaps not clearly articulated, lies at the root of the many tribal wars and of much cruelty. The most notable victims of this belief have been the Jews, a race of people whom God has selected to fulfil a special role in his plan and whom, in spite of almost ceaseless persecutions, he has preserved in order to ensure that the defeat of Satan may be complete. This belief has been most horrifically expressed in the Holocaust, in which the Nazis massacred 6 million Jews, but variants of it have been used throughout history to persecute one of the most peace-loving races in the world. A particular variant that has persisted for 2,000 years is the belief that the Jews were responsible for the crucifixion of Christ and should therefore be restrained if not punished with death. This led to their being the main victims of the Inquisition.

The belief that remission of time in Purgatory can be bought is a curious example of Satan's wiles. It was seized on by Inquisitors in the fifteenth and sixteenth centuries to extract money from a largely illiterate and credulous peasantry by the sale of indulgences, and was almost certainly not held to be true by those who administered the system. Their error in pretending that the remission of sins is a commercial matter was almost certainly more reprehensible than the sins committed by their victims, whose gifts they hoped would enrich their church and possibly also themselves.

The false belief that the soul is not primarily a combatant in the war between good and evil, but rather a battleground on which the war is conducted by two equal or nearly equal gods, has a long history. There seems to be an innate propensity in the human mind to see the affairs of the world in terms of a conflict between opposing forces. This propensity probably lies at the root of Hegel's 'thesis and antithesis', which, when applied by Karl Marx to social and economic affairs, gave rise to the evils of communism. It is central to the ethics of Zoroaster (*c*. 600 BC), who taught that Ormuzd (or Ahura Mazda), the Spirit of good, is constantly at war with Ahriman, the Spirit of evil, but will ultimately triumph. The danger lying in all theories of opposing deities is that if these are both credited with creative powers, they inevitably lead to the belief that the material world, including the human body, was created by the lesser (evil) deity and is therefore intrinsically evil, with disastrous consequences for the formulation of a true moral theory. This false belief, which has already been mentioned on pages 68–9, is contrary to the teaching of Christianity and of most other religions and must be firmly resisted.

About 250 years ago Satan planted the seeds of three false beliefs which since then he has assiduously fed and watered. For his purpose he sought the most fertile ground for these seeds and found it in the souls and minds of those living in the Western world, where they have flourished and grown into certainties that few people have thought of questioning, although recently some doubting voices have been raised. Satan has been aided in establishing these beliefs by the fact that they all share the characteristic, mentioned on pages 81–82, of containing a measure of truth.

The first belief, already mentioned briefly on page 16, is that in order to build the kingdom of God on earth it is necessary to increase to the maximum the production of wealth. It is important to emphasise that what is here condemned is not the acquisition of wealth, although this, if not controlled by submission to God's will, can be an obstacle to personal salvation, as Christ pointed out on several occasions (Matthew vi, 19, 20, 24; xix, 21, 24). What is condemned here is the error that wealth is the key to the salvation of humankind. This is the error refuted by Paul in his statement to Timothy that 'the love of money is the root of all evil' (1 Timothy vi, 10). It is of course obvious that, although complete equality of income throughout the whole world is neither attainable nor desirable, the disparity of the standard of living between the richest and the poorest countries of the world is indefensible, and it is easy for Satan to suggest that this disparity will be eliminated by increasing wealth. If the provision of food, clothing, shelter and useful employment is the objective sought and if the production of wealth contributes and is directed to this end, it is good, but Satan has perverted this truth by persuading us that *therefore* the production of wealth, as an end in itself, should be our primary objective.

The second false belief is that, whatever ills may befall humankind, science will find a way of overcoming them. Although we shall find that this is not true, the roots from which it springs contain a substantial measure of truth. For scientific inquiry, which has as its target the discovery of the laws which God has implanted in the universe of both living and non-living creatures, is essentially good. Scientific research must therefore be supported and encouraged, and this duty is generally accepted and put into practice in those parts of the world that can afford it, the support being given by both government and industry. The reason for this support, however, is seldom that science can reveal part of God's essence, but rather that it can confer benefits on humankind, and has done so during the past 150 years to a very marked degree. The most obvious of these benefits is in the understanding of the causes of, and in finding cures for, many diseases. This has been so marked that it is not surprising that we should feel justified in extending the beneficial and curative powers of science to cover all the evils with which humankind is confronted, whether economic, social, pathological (whether physico – or psycho-) or criminological. This belief is, however, erroneous, and if persisted in will reveal its falsity in ways that will probably be very unpleasant. The remedy for human ills lies in submission to the will of God, in allowing the Holy Spirit to cleanse the channel of obligation so that Christ can come and dwell in us. In this, science has an important part to play, but it is only a part, not the whole.

Satan's objective in instilling these false beliefs is to degrade the human mind and to render it more responsive to his persuasions. The third false belief is the most efficacious in promoting this objective, and the most rapid in action, and there is evidence that he regards it as his favourite device, for he certainly uses it very extensively. It also has the advantage, from his point of view, of being more easily fostered because of his success in persuading us to adopt the second belief. For the fact that we regard science as omnipotent has led to the advances in knowledge on which the third belief rests. This is the belief that if a new technological device can be shown to improve our standard of living, or to be beneficial to humankind in any way, then it ought to be adopted and developed to the fullest extent possible. This is sometimes expressed in the wider form that all progress, or at least all technological progress, is beneficial and should be promoted, or in the crude aphorism 'you cannot halt progress'.

The main technological developments of the past hundred years have been the telephone, the internal-combustion engine, jet propulsion, the aeroplane and helicopter, the discovery of the structure of the atom, the discovery of the genetic basis governing the characteristics, both physical and psychological, of all living beings, the expansion of the chemical industry and its application to agriculture, radio, television, the computer, virtual reality and the Internet. All these can be shown to have conferred benefits on humankind, but only two, the telephone and radio, are relatively innocuous. All the others contain the seeds of calamitous events and, taken in conjunction, may even threaten the survival of humanity on earth.

The reason why a warning against the probable consequences of these technological developments must be given is that we do not rule them, they rule us. They have become the idols of the twentieth century, akin to and replacing the idols whose worship is repeatedly condemned in the historical and prophetical books of the Old Testament, as being in breach of the first and greatest Commandment: 'I am the Lord thy God, thou shalt have no other gods before me' (Exodus xx, 2, 3). Even more tellingly, we may identify these rulers of our lives with the kings condemned by Hosea: 'They have set up kings, but not by me; they have made princes and I knew it not; of their silver and gold they have made idols, that they may be cut off... Mine anger is kindled against them; how long will it be ere they attain to innocency?' (Hosea viii, 4, 5). For our error lies not so much in having discovered the means of making these technological advances, but in adopting them and putting them to work for us without first consulting God in prayer, in earnest, prolonged and soul-searching prayer. Again, it must be pointed out that prayer does not consist of beating one's breast and bemoaning one's sins (for this can become a luxury) but in earnest seeking to discover God's will and constantly bearing in mind the reason for our creation (see pages 71-2).

The attack on false beliefs on pages 81-7 may lead some readers to hold me guilty of illogicality or even hypocrisy. They may argue that in condemning these beliefs I am falling into the same error as that described on pages 82-3, the error of outlawing those who hold them. I think, however, that such a judgment would be invalid. In condemning false beliefs, what is claimed is that by holding them and putting them into practice we are allowing Satan to gain a victory over us (though only a temporary victory), and delaying the building of God's kingdom. It is not claimed that those who hold one or more of these beliefs are thereby imperilling their immortal souls. This, on the other hand, is precisely what is claimed by those who believe that to them alone (and to their sect) has divine revelation been vouchsafed. In fact, God alone can know to what extent the soul of any individual is damaged by holding a particular belief (as to doctrine or otherwise) or by failing to resist and condemn a false belief held by the greater part of society in which he or she lives. The condemnation of false beliefs and the requirement to accept the truth of certain doctrines on pain of damnation are therefore quite distinct.

Another criticism that may be levelled against the condemnation of false beliefs is that not everyone is convinced that they are false and that everyone is entitled to his or her opinion. Freedom of thought, as well as freedom of speech and action within the law, is regarded as a basic right that should not be infringed. Due weight must be given to this presumed right, but it is not unqualified. For truth is an absolute, dwelling in God, and to oppose it is blasphemy. False beliefs may, of course, be trivial, and it would be foolish to take exception to these. No great harm is done if someone maintains that the world is flat; and if the theory is advanced, and supported by evidence, that the early plays of Shakespeare were written by Elizabeth I and the remainder by James I, the only consequence would be a highly entertaining squabble between scholars.

Beliefs as to the duties and the destiny of humankind are, however, in a different category. They are supremely important, and if those we hold are false the consequences could be disastrous. We are therefore under an obligation to ensure, so far as is possible, that the beliefs falling in this category and held by the majority of people are true. In this chapter I have condemned a number of beliefs and in doing so I have, of course, been expressing my own opinions. It is open to others to disagree, but I have no doubt that evidence will be forthcoming in due course to support my thesis, and that this evidence will be so strong that it can be ignored only by those whom Satan has firmly in his grip.

I put forward one further suggestion about Satan's weaponry which I hold to be probably true, but not with the certainty expressed above in relation to false beliefs. I have suggested (on page 74) that Satan can use his miraculous powers to create or modify viruses to attack our bodies. These are, of course, physical viruses, and it is sometimes possible to ward against them by injecting suitable vaccines. It is, however, probable that Satan also has the power to create psychical viruses, which can spread like an epidemic through a whole community, or a whole nation, or even through several nations, rendering the people who are attacked by them susceptible to brainwashing, so that a false and possibly evil belief may be accepted as true by a whole population. The present century has provided examples of this which render the hypothesis very credible. If such viruses exist, the reason why they have not been detected is that their substance (see page 34) is mental substance, which is not detectable by any scientific process known to us.

In so far as we perform satisfactorily the duties imposed on us in the war with Satan, we are not only contributing to building the kingdom of God on earth, we are also cleansing our souls of their imperfections. We cannot reach perfection and God does not expect us to do so, but his assessment of our success while on earth will depend on the extent to which we have resisted Satan's attempts to persuade us to close the channel of obligation and have allowed Christ to enter our souls to guide them towards perfection. In other words, the test theory discussed in Chapter I, though incomplete, is true and must be given due weight.

God knows, however, that few of us will have made enough progress towards perfection during earthly life to be allowed to assume the further responsibilities of eternal life. Before we can attain this ultimate goal we shall need further training and further insight into our relation to and our duty to God. For this purpose we are promised that after death we shall be given a new span of temporal life, in a new dimension, in which to receive this training and enlightenment. We should look forward to this gift as an occasion for thanksgiving and praise, for as our training progresses, the performance of our duties, which at present we may find onerous, will become enjoyable.

All Christians and all Muslims believe that life does not end with earthly death, and the same is true of most Jews (see Daniel xii, 1–4, John xi, 24, and Matthew xxii, 23–32) and of many who belong to other faiths. We do not know what happens at the moment of death, but we are entitled to speculate; indeed, we are under a duty to do so in order to prepare ourselves for the life that lies ahead, and in the following paragraphs I put forward some suggestions in an attempt to discharge this duty.

When we die, the accidents (see page 34) of our bodies are buried or cremated and cease to play any part in our journey towards heaven. The substance of our bodies, however, with all the characteristics, both good and evil, it has acquired during life on earth, is preserved. This substance, previously the substance of physical being, is transformed by the soul into mental substance, and takes up its abode in eternity together with the soul, which has always dwelt there. The soul, the mind and the body will thus be even more closely linked than before death; together they will form a trinity in unity, sharing eternal being.

The ultimate objective which God has ordained for them, and which will be attained if they submit themselves wholly to his will, is that they should all share not only eternal being but also eternal life, that is to say, life which, once attained, is no longer dependent on God's sustaining activity and can only be annihilated by a positive act of God. Eternal life, however, will not be attained until God is satisfied that our particular role in the war with Satan has been completely fulfilled.

In the interim we, having eternal being and temporal life, and dwelling in eternity, will remain after death in contact with the world of time and space, and will be required to use our powers to guide the souls of those who are on earth along the right path. Satan will, of course, continue his evil attempts to subvert our wills, and it is probable that, as we shall be ontologically on an exact par with him, his attacks will be different from and even fiercer than those we have to repel while on earth. It would, however, be pointless to speculate on the temptations we shall have to conquer and the problems we shall have to solve in the second stage of our journey to God. Christ himself has told us 'to take no thought for the morrow; for the morrow shall take thought for the things of itself. Sufficient unto the day is the evil thereof' (Matthew vi, 34).

God's Interventions

God is, of course, constantly intervening to ensure that we shall ultimately succeed in defeating Satan and thereby laying the foundation for restoring harmony to heaven and for the further work that has to be accomplished there. Two instances of his intervention, one positive and one negative, have already been mentioned. He has intervened, and continues to intervene, negatively by imposing restraints on the power of our souls to perform miracles. This restraint is imposed because, in our present state of immaturity, we would certainly use this power unwisely; we may expect, therefore, that it will be relaxed as we grow in wisdom. The second intervention by God, which is also continuously in action, is his readiness to respond positively to a sincere plea for guidance. We must not, however, expect this response to be given unless the plea is genuine. If our request is for his approval of whatever we are doing, a response will not be forthcoming unless what we are doing is right in his eyes. All such requests must be accompanied by an expression of repentance – that is, of *metanoia*, a willingness to change our course of action if it is wrong.

These two interventions, however, though continuous, would not suffice to enable us to fulfil the purpose for which we were created, if they were not supported by the unique and most powerful intervention of all, the Incarnation of God in Jesus Christ. This intervention was described in the opening words of this book as the central event in the history of the human race, and this description must now be justified by an attempt to assess, as precisely as possible, what Jesus accomplished by his life, his death and his resurrection on earth, and his ascension into heaven.

God knew, from the beginning, before time and space were created, that his incarnation as a human being would be an unavoidable consequence of the expression of his essence as love. It is possible that he has also undergone other incarnations in various parts of the universe where he has found it necessary to create temporal beings to contribute to the fulfilment of his purpose. It is necessary to mention this, lest we should become too arrogant by believing that we are the only soldiers in God's army, but it would be pointless to pursue this possibility further.

It was necessary, not only that God should become incarnate in Jesus Christ, but that the fact that he had done so should be convincingly made known to the world. To his disciples and a few others, his own words and actions were sufficient for this purpose; John records that, when speaking to those who he knew would be receptive, he repeatedly proclaimed his close relationship to, even his unity with, the Father. Out of many examples, four will suffice to make good this claim. 'I am the way, the truth, and the life; no man cometh unto the Father, but by me' (John xiv, 6); 'He that hath seen me hath seen the Father' (John xiv, 9); 'Believe me that I am in the Father and the Father in me' (John xiv, 11); 'I and the Father are one' (John x, 30). And in his prayer to the Father for the apostles who would be entrusted with the responsibility of spreading the gospel he said 'Holy Father, keep through thine own name those whom thou has given me, that they may be one, as we are' (John xvii, 11). And later in the same prayer he extended this petition to all those who would come to believe in him: 'Neither pray I for these alone, but for them also which shall believe on me through their word; that they all may be one; as thou Father art in me, and I in thee, that they also may be one in us; that the world may believe that thou has sent me' (John xvii, 20, 21).

His disciples were no doubt at first confused. They found his personality so compelling that (at least for much of their time) they left their homes and their work to travel round Galilee, Samaria and Judaea with him. They knew that many people, especially those whom he had healed of some disease, were speculating about him and wondering who he was, some confusing him with John the Baptist – Herod even thought that John had risen from the dead (Matthew xiv, 2) – others saying that he was a reincarnation of Elijah or Jeremiah (Matthew xvi, 14). Gradually, however, they came to recognise his true identity, culminating in Peter's triumphant statement 'Thou art the Christ, the Son of the living God' (Matthew xvi, 16). Others also recognised him, even before the Resurrection, as divine. Thus Martha, when she sought Jesus to ask him to cure her brother Lazarus, said 'Lord, I believe that thou art the Christ, the Son of God' (John xi, 27). And on the Cross, the penitent malefactor who was crucified with Jesus recognised that he had divine authority, saying 'Lord, remember me when thou comest into thy kingdom' (Luke xxiii, 39–43).

All these people, however, except the last mentioned, knew Jesus well; they had heard his preaching and had seen the miracles he had performed. In order to convince others of his generation and, even more importantly, succeeding generations, that he was the Son of God incarnate in human flesh, something more dramatic was required. The fact that he did not have an earthly father would certainly not have sufficed, even if people could be convinced that it was true. It is indeed questionable whether the disciples took much note of this fact; there is certainly no record in the gospels that it was ever adduced during the course of his ministry as proof of his divinity. It is true that both Matthew and Luke record the virgin birth in their gospels, but these were written several years after the Resurrection.

Miraculous healings and other miracles would also have been inadequate to establish his claim to divinity. In the course of his ministry Jesus performed many miracles – turning water into wine (John ii, 1–10), calming the storm (Matthew viii, 24–27), healing a nobleman's son (John iv, 46–54), a cripple (John v, 2–9), a blind man (John ix, 1–7) and countless other people, as recorded in the synoptic gospels, feeding a multitude with a few loaves and fishes (John vi, 1–14; Mark viii, 1–9), raising Lazarus to life (John xi, 17–44), also the son of a widow of Nain (Luke vii, 11–17) and

Jairus's daughter (Mark v, 22–43), and walking on the water (John vi, 16–21). But although these aroused wonder they were certainly not regarded as proof of his divinity. For both Elijah and Elisha had performed miracles similar to those performed by Jesus. The feeding of the five thousand is paralleled by the case of the widow of Zarephath, who had in her home only a handful of flour and a small jug of oil, but these remained undiminished and fed her, her family and Elijah during a prolonged drought. And when her son died Elijah raised him to life (1 Kings xvii, 7–24). Elisha performed a similar miracle for a destitute widow who had only a small jar of oil and was being dunned by her creditors. He increased the oil to fill several jars, which she sold to pay her debts (2 Kings iv, 1–7). He also cleansed Naaman of leprosy (2 Kings v, 1–14) and raised to life the son of a Shunamite woman (2 Kings iv, 8–36). But these miracles did not lead to either Elijah or Elisha's being regarded as divine. The ancient Jews expected their holy men and women to be able to perform miracles. We may recall that when Aaron was commanded by Pharaoh to perform a miracle he cast his staff on the ground and it became a snake (Exodus vii, 8), and that when the Israelites were thirsting in the wilderness, Moses struck a rock and water gushed forth from it (Numbers xx, 11). Even the defiance of gravity shown by Jesus walking on the water was not without precedent, for when a borrowed axe-head accidentally fell into the Jordan, Elisha caused it to float (2 Kings vi, 5–7).

According to Luke's record (Luke xxiv, 50–53; Acts i, 9–11) the ascension of Jesus was witnessed only by the disciples, to whom he had appeared many times after his resurrection, and who already acknowledged him to be the Son of God. But this event, even if witnessed by many other people, would have been regarded as an act of God, showing his approval of a very holy man, not as evidence of that man's divinity. Not having known Jesus personally, and being unaware that he had died and risen from the grave (or, if they had heard of the Resurrection, did not believe that it had really occurred), they would have put him in the same category as Enoch, who without having died a natural death was taken by God (Genesis v, 24), or Elijah, who was taken by a whirlwind into heaven (2 Kings ii, 11).

Thus, in order to establish his credentials as the Son of God it was necessary for him to die and to rise from the dead. Nothing less would have sufficed. It was by preaching the Resurrection of Jesus that the early apostles were able to spread the gospel so powerfully and so rapidly that by the end of the first century Christian communities had been established in many parts of the Roman Empire, and towards the end of the second century Tertullian was able to claim that the gospel had been preached 'all over the world, from Egypt to Morocco, from Iran to Spain, from the south Russian steppe to Britain'*.

It was also necessary that Jesus should suffer a violent death at the hand of the ruling authority. For God intended that the Resurrection should not only attest to the fact that in Jesus he was incarnated in human flesh and that he had power over death, he also intended that it should establish his power over all earthly authority, however great. At the Transfiguration (Mark ix, 2–8) Moses and Elijah were present with Jesus, and the disciples, though terrified, did not regard their presence as revealing any truth that had hitherto been concealed from them. The same would have been the case if Jesus, after a natural death, had later appeared to his disciples. They would have been amazed; but they were accustomed to being amazed by him, and his appearance would have confirmed their belief in a life after death, but it would not have given them the power to convince others of his divinity which they displayed after the actual Resurrection, as Luke has recorded in the Acts of the Apostles. This power was, of course, the gift of the Holy Spirit, but it is clear from the prophecies of his death and resurrection made by Christ in the course of his mission that it was necessary for him to be condemned to death by the greatest earthly authority ever known in order that his resur-

---

Early Christianity, edited by Ian Hazlett, SPCK, 1991, page 69.

rection should prove that even that authority was powerless to frustrate God's purpose.

It remains to state, with as much precision as is possible in this difficult field, what God has accomplished and what he has done for us by his incarnation in Jesus Christ, and by Christ's teaching, his crucifixion and his resurrection. Although preachers often speak with great assurance on this matter, telling us that Christ, by his death and resurrection, has atoned for our sins, they seldom explain what this means. We must not criticize them for this failure, for the full meaning of God's intervention is obscure, and in our present state of immaturity our understanding of this mystery can be no more than partial. We may, however, expect that, as Christ has promised (John xvi, 12, 13), as we become more mature, and have begun to make some real progress in the task of building his kingdom on earth, we shall be more fully enlightened. In the meantime we must do our best to understand what the scriptures reveal to us, and to carry out his instruction to preach the gospel throughout the world (Matthew xxviii, 19).

Christ himself has given us few clues. As already noted (page 7), he spent most of his time travelling and teaching, mainly in parables, explaining the meaning of the commandment to love one's neighbour, describing the kingdom of heaven, again in parables (Matthew xiii, 24–52), and healing the sick. He forgave sins (Matthew ix, 2; Luke vii, 48), and after his resurrection he gave his disciples power to remit sins (John xx, 22). However, although we can learn much from all these events, they do not reveal the full reason of his coming to earth and undergoing a cruel death. There are, however, other statements made by Jesus that throw more light on this question. 'The Son of man is come to save that which is lost' (Matthew xviii, 11); and again 'I am not come to call the righteous but sinners to repentance' (Matthew ix, 13). All these events took place before the Crucifixion, and Jesus did not relate his acts and statements to his death and resurrection. It is indeed obvious that God has power to forgive sins and that this power is not in any way dependent on the death of his Son on the Cross.

Jesus did, however, on a few occasions link his death with

the need of humankind for forgiveness and salvation. He told Nicodemus that 'God sent not his Son into the world to condemn the world, but that the world through him might be saved' (John iii, 17). He also said 'The Son of man came not to be ministered unto, but to minister, and to give his life a ransom for many' (Matthew xx, 28). Even more explicitly, at the Last Supper he said 'This is my blood of the new testament, which is shed for many for the remission of sins' (Matthew xxvi, 28).

The main testimony to the connection between Christ's mission on earth and the sinfulness of humankind is not, however, to be found in his own words, but in those of the angels who appeared to Joseph in a dream, to John the disciple of Jesus, John the Baptist and Paul. Matthew records that the angel told Joseph that Mary, who was betrothed to him, was pregnant, and said 'That which is conceived in her is of the Holy Ghost, and she shall bring forth a son, and thou shalt call his name Jesus, for he shall save his people from their sins' (Matthew i, 20, 21). Thirty years later, when John the Baptist saw Jesus approaching, he said 'Behold the Lamb of God, which taketh away the sin of the world' (John i, 29). Paul in his epistles frequently refers to the redemptive power of the death of Jesus on the Cross, and John tells us that 'the blood of Jesus cleanseth us from all sin' (1 John i, 7). Probably the most familiar references are 'This is a true saying and worthy of all men to be believed, that Christ Jesus came into the world to save sinners'* (1 Timothy i, 15), and 'If any man sin, we have an advocate with the Father, Jesus Christ the righteous, and he is the propitiation for our sins' (1 John ii, 1, 2).

These and other similar statements in the New Testament tell us that the impact of our sinfulness on our ultimate destiny has been lessened or in some other way modified by Christ's death and resurrection, but the manner in which this has been and is still being done is not easy to discover. In our

---

*The wording used here is that of the 1662 *Book of Common Prayer*.

effort to resolve this mystery we must start by noting that the remission (or forgiveness – in the Authorised version of the Bible the Greek word *aphesis* is translated by both these words) of sin does not mean that the temporal consequences of sin are annulled. It is obvious that this must be so because, as we have seen (page 67), it is part of God's plan that we should learn from our mistakes. Only thus can we be trained to become efficient soldiers in God's army. God may in his mercy modify the most damaging consequences of our errors, lest we should lose heart, but we cannot escape the necessity of learning how to repel Satan's unceasing onslaughts, and this lesson can only be learned by experience. The damage may be largely, though probably not completely, avoided by repentance, provided that this is sincere, involving a determination by the soul as well as by the mind to reject the sin. But we cannot rely on Christ's sacrifice to annul the consequences of our sins, or to relieve us of our responsibility for them. The truth of this is attested by all experience. If someone commits a sin, say by striking another person in a fit of temper and without just cause, the consequence is resentment and a desire for revenge, the souls of both the attacker and the victim are damaged, and much suffering, involving possibly many other people, will be caused. Only a sincere attempt at reconciliation can reduce, much less repair, the damage, and even this will seldom obliterate the incident from the memories of those concerned. We can go further, for not only are the temporal consequences of sin not annulled by Christ's death on the Cross; full repentance is also necessary before we can enter on eternal life.

The fact that remission (or forgiveness) does not entail annihilation of the consequences of sin is even more clearly seen where the sin is communal, the adoption by a whole community of a false belief, leading to the pursuit by that community of wrong objectives. When this occurs, the communal soul will give birth to faculties by which, and create conditions in which, those objectives can be brought to fruition, with disastrous results. In the Western world we have, during the past 250 years, wrongly allowed economic considerations to dominate our lives, we have accepted every technological advance without reference to God's will, and we have sought to promote what has seemed to us to be 'the greatest happiness of the greatest number', which has often meant providing the means to satisfy worthless or at best trivial interests. And we have done all these things with little regard to the well-being of posterity. The catastrophes that will flow from this gigantic communal sin are beginning to be seen all around us, and are daily looming larger. We shall certainly be led to repent of these sins, in the sense of being sorry that we committed them, but much more than this will be required to repair the damage that will have been done. Nothing less than *metanoia*, a complete change of outlook and objective, will suffice, and we shall soon be forced to take this drastic step. In the meantime we shall have to endure the consequences of what we have done.

These will be devastating and will involve much suffering. It will suffice to name a few. The problem of unemployment, disastrous for the young, creating the belief that they are of no value to society and therefore also of no value to God, will remain insoluble, and may even become more acute. This evil, coupled with the debasement of art, is a large factor in the rise of the drug culture, which is destroying the bodies, minds and souls of so many adolescents. The increasing use of chemicals in agriculture, based on the false belief that every hectare of land must be forced to yield the maximum quantity of food (while at the same time farmers are being compelled to set aside land for non-agricultural purposes) is poisoning our rivers and oceans, and the pollution of the atmosphere by the apparently uncontrollable reliance on the internal-combustion engine is a major cause of the increase in respiratory diseases. It is also a contributory cause, though probably not the only cause, of global warming, the full consequences of which are at present unpredictable but are certainly alarming. We are told that, as a result of this change in the world's climate, brought about by our folly, 'Southern Africa is facing a catastrophe of unprecedented proportions, according to scientists who predict a drought lasting for 100 years'*.

More ominous than any of these is our misuse of the knowledge we have gained into the structure of the atom. It is hardly too much to say that as a result of this sinful folly our present way of life will, but for the grace of God, become a way of death. For it is axiomatic that all human artefacts are imperfect. It follows that so long as we rely on nuclear power to supply our needs for energy there will be accidents. These may be rare, and some may not be very severe, but cumulatively the consequences will inevitably be disastrous. There is also the problem of the disposal of nuclear waste. The half-life of some radioactive elements is 20,000 years, and no matter what steps are taken to prevent the escape of radiation, we cannot know what changes will take place in the structure of the earth while this waste is still active. Whether we bury it on land or at sea, it may come to the surface while still powerfully active, and it is a cardinal sin to expose posterity to such danger. Nor can we salve our consciences by projecting the waste into space, for after ten or a hundred or even a thousand years it may land on a planet in our or another galaxy on which God, in pursuance of his purpose, has created life.

There is, of course, also the danger of a third world war, in which nuclear weapons will cause such widespread devastation that the human race will be wiped out and a large part of the earth rendered uninhabitable for thousands of years. We need not, however, devote much thought to this possibility, for it is certain that God will not allow his plan for the defeat and redemption of Satan to be completely frustrated by our folly. We may be certain that before the downward course of events becomes irreversible he will intervene to prevent an uncontrollable disaster.

If the forgiveness or remission of sin, which Christ secured for us by his death, does not relieve us of the adverse consequences that all sin entails, what meaning can be attached to

---

The Times, 18 October 1995.

the promise given by the angel to Joseph, or the other statements quoted above (page 97). The answer is to be found in the last of those quotations – not, however, as there rendered but in the new rendering which is adopted in recent translations of the New Testament. For the word 'propitiation' is misleading; it conjures up the vision of a vengeful God, angrily demanding that someone must suffer for our wrongdoing, and refusing to relent until he has been appeased. The modern rendering is 'expiation' or 'atonement', and of these the latter gives us the most easily explained and the most accurate description of what Christ has achieved for us, provided we give to 'atonement' its true meaning 'restoration of unity with' (at-one-ment). What Christ has done is not to placate an angry Father, but to ensure that our sinfulness will not break our link with the Father. His action is directed to repairing us, not to placating God. We are linked to God by the channel or bond of obligation, and every sin we commit creates a blockage in this channel. But Christ has ensured that, however many obstacles we create, we cannot close it entirely. The bond cannot be broken, and the Holy Spirit can always cleanse it, if we will allow him to do so. We do not know how this remedial and safeguarding action is brought about by Christ's death, and it would be pointless to speculate. For it is an event in eternity, and the laws of cause and effect in eternity are different from those in the temporal order with which we are familiar. What we are required to do is to believe; God will do the rest.

The meaning of the Cross is manifold, but this aspect is important, and we must try to understand precisely the nature of the boon it confers. It does not mean that God will ensure that everyone will attain eternal life; it means that the opportunity to be thus blessed will never be withdrawn. The final decision rests with every individual person. The option is given to everyone, whether Christian, Jew, Muslim, Buddhist, Hindu, Sikh or Jain, or a member of any other religious group. It is given to those who have never heard of the Holy Spirit or of Christ, and is not withheld even from those who claim to be agnostics or atheists. For adherence to a particular creed is largely a matter of accepting, intellectually, a doctrinal explanation of the mysteries of life and death, and a particular belief in how the universe is governed, whether this is by purpose, inexorable law or randomness, or any combination of these. But the opening of the channel of obligation is a spiritual determination, taking place in the soul, and may be completely unrecognised or misunderstood by the intellect. Thus although God will not allow sin, however great, to sever or even to block completely the channel which is our link with him, it remains the responsibility of the individual, by a sincere repentance, to invite the Holy Spirit to enter. Failure to take this final step, even though God will wait patiently until the end of time, is the sin against the Holy Spirit, which Christ has told us is the only sin that will not be forgiven (Matthew xii, 31, 32).

The remission of sin by Christ's death, as interpreted above, is obviously a gift of inestimable value to every human being. The assurance that our link with God will not be completely severed by sin testifies to God's love, and is a blessing which every individual person is invited to accept and enjoy, but it is not the only blessing that God has conferred on us by the life, death and resurrection of his Son. He is not only concerned that salvation should be available to everyone, he is also determined that the human race, working not as a collection of individuals each seeking his or her own well-being, but as an army under orders, seeking to know his will and fighting the enemy in comradeship, shall not fail him. For we are told 'he hath called us with an holy calling, not according to our works, but according to his own purpose and grace, which was given us in Christ Jesus before the world began. But is now made manifest by the appearing of our Saviour Jesus Christ, who hath abolished death, and hath brought life and immortality to light through the gospel' (2 Timothy i, 9, 10).

This statement confirms that we, the whole human race, are engaged in a crusade, we have been created to fulfil a definite purpose; it also confirms that eternal life is within the grasp of everyone. Its meaning is, however, wider than is conveyed by these assurances. For the abolition or conquest of death tells us more than that we shall survive earthly death. This was already a tenet of many Eastern religions and was widely accepted by Jews and others, including Greeks, before Christ appeared on earth. The conquest of death is an affirmation, never to be doubted or even questioned, that in the war with Satan we shall be victorious; that, however many setbacks we may have to endure and however grievous their consequences, Satan will finally surrender (cf. page 72). For if it were otherwise, if Satan should triumph, he would destroy the human race; God would then have to abandon his strategy to use us as a battalion in his army and devise a new strategy to restore harmony to heaven by the defeat and redemption of the rebellious angels.

We know therefore that the conquest of death revealed by Paul to Timothy means that God has taken positive action to ensure that Satan cannot ultimately prevail. We do not know precisely how he has done this, but a clue is given by the Apostles' Creed, in which it is affirmed, as an article of faith, that Christ, in the time between his death and his resurrection, descended into hell. This, of course, is an allegorical statement, for hell is not a place; its meaning is that he encountered Satan face to face, and partially disarmed him. The most probable interpretation of this mystery is that he deprived Satan of the eternal life which, together with all angels, he had enjoyed up to that moment. Satan was, and still is, endowed with eternal being, but his life has been reduced from the eternal to the temporal mode, dependent on God's continuing sustaining activity. He is therefore ontologically on a par with our souls before they, having completed their mission (possibly after several reincarnations) attain to eternal life. Moreover, although his powers of deception remain active, he can no longer use them to persuade us that, if we agree to be guided by him, we shall attain that goal, because the concept of eternal life is now beyond his comprehension. Our task of defeating him is thus rendered easier.

What the Incarnation of God in Christ has accomplished for us can therefore be summarised in two sentences. First, it has assured us that eternal life is within our grasp if we allow the Holy Spirit to cleanse our link with God and admit Christ to direct the course both of our daily lives and of our evolution.

And secondly, it has given us the assurance that, guided by God, we shall defeat Satan and build the kingdom of God on earth. In this kingdom the three cardinal virtues of faith, hope, and charity (agape) will prevail, but in order to achieve the destiny which was designed for us before the beginning of time we need to cultivate these virtues now. From them we shall derive the courage that will be needed to enable us to overcome the immense difficulties that lie ahead, difficulties and problems arising from our past and present folly in allowing Satan to dictate so many of our beliefs and objectives, as outlined earlier in this chapter. The fact that we have allowed ourselves to be thus misled is daily being revealed in the growth of social and ecological evils and in the instability of the two major economic systems of the world. These evils cannot easily be reversed and are bound to lead to a series of calamities, which will be sufficiently devastating to compel us to direct our development into a new course. They will not, however, overwhelm us, for God will not allow Satan to tempt us beyond what we can bear (1 Corinthians x, 13), and by faith we shall be buoyed up by the certainty of ultimate victory.

The partial disarming of Satan by depriving him of eternal life was the greatest sacrifice made by God in the crucifixion and resurrection of his Son. For eternal life is a gift in which some part of the essence of God is implanted in the recipient, and the deprivation of eternal life therefore has the effect of rendering inactive some part of God's essence. This is not a trivial matter, for the measure of eternal life is infinite. There are many degrees of infinity and the infinity of the eternal life of a created being is small in relation to that of God himself; but it is nevertheless an infinity and if it were annihilated a small part of God himself would be destroyed. Eternal life should not be regarded as a fully ripened gift; it is a seed containing an element of God which the recipient is under a duty to nourish and bring to fruition (cf. Matthew xxv, 14–30). We have already seen (pages 24–25) that God will not destroy anything that he has created so long as any possibility remains of its redemption. Still less is he willing to destroy any part of himself. From this it follows that the eternal life which Satan enjoyed before the resurrection of Christ and which is part of God's essence, is held in reserve, to be restored to Satan when he repents. These considerations provide a further proof that we shall, in the fulness of time, win the war with Satan and build God's kingdom on earth.

One final point remains to be made. I have said that, as Satan no longer enjoys eternal life, he is unable to entertain the concept of this mode of life and cannot convey that concept to us. It might be argued that our souls, having the same ontological status as Satan (eternal being and temporal life), are also unable to entertain the concept of eternal life. This, however, is a false argument. For the ability to entertain, and in some measure to understand, a spiritual concept depends not only on ontological status but also on relationship with God. Satan, having rebelled against God, has no link with him. We, on the other hand, have not rebelled, although we have allowed ourselves to be led into false paths, and too many of our prayers end with the unspoken words 'nevertheless, not thy will, but mine, be done'. Our link with God remains unbroken, and consequently the concept of eternal life is potentially within our comprehension. Our understanding is still rudimentary, but we know that eternal life is 'more abundant' (John x, 10) than temporal life. We also know that when we attain to eternal life we will not be perfect, but our souls will be striving to attune themselves with the will of God. And to crown these elements of our understanding we know that in eternal life we shall be one with Christ. For in the Resurrection Christ did not discard his earthly body and mind; the accidents of his earthly body were destroyed (hence the empty tomb), but the substance was transformed into mental substance, his earthly will, always in harmony with his divine will, was united with it, and the spiritual body, mind and soul thus created, ascended into heaven forty days after the Resurrection to be united with his Father. From this we learn that, as we shall resemble Christ in having a spiritual body and mind, united with our souls, we will be wholly regenerate and, by adoption and grace, will become the children of God.

4

Implications, Inferences and Initial Steps

The Kingdom of God

It has already been stated (pages 67 and 98) that in the war against Satan our training is accomplished by our learning from our mistakes. Our choice and pursuit of wrong objectives must in all cases inevitably lead to disaster, although the full measure of the disaster may be delayed, and in the early stages our blindness may conceal from us the link between our folly and its consequences. The errors we have committed during the past 250 years – amplified and pursued with redoubled vigour during the past 100 years – will lead, at some time during the twenty-first century, and probably during its first half, to a number of calamities, ecological, economic, demographic and social, which will be sufficiently severe to make us realise our folly; but by the mercy of God will not cause us to lose hope for recovery and a better future for humankind (cf. 1 Corinthians x, 13). The whole population of the world will be in a state of great confusion, and there may be a period of some years in which we will flounder in uncertainty, but gradually we shall begin on the task of stabilising the conditions of life and of realising that the task for which we were created, that of defeating Satan and building the kingdom of God on earth, must be resumed. We shall learn not to make the mistake of supposing that we know what the kingdom of God will be like, of creating in our minds visions of utopias which, like the vision that we in the last years of the twentieth century hold, will prove to be false and leading only to disaster. We shall begin to understand that we must leave it to God to reveal the conditions that will prevail in his kingdom and pray, sincerely and unceasingly, for enlightenment, and we may be certain that this will be given when the time is ripe for us to receive it. With this certainty hope will be renewed and we shall embark on our task with vigour and with greater reliance on God's providence than before the disasters consequent on our present follies.

We know that the kingdom of God is not fully attainable on earth, since men and women are not perfect and are not perfectible. We also know that, after we have recovered from the initial confusion and have made progress along the right path, the kingdom can and will be approached asymptotically (page 65). It cannot be described in a single phrase, for it is a complex of many features ('In my house are many mansions' – John xiv, 2), and progress may be made towards building some of these features while movement on others may be slow or even retrogressive. Even when the human race as a whole is pressing forward in the right direction, there will be some who will resist. Those who have an axe to grind or have a vested interest in maintaining the *status quo* will try to persuade us that things are all right as they are and that what is needed is more of the same instead of a new beginning. Progress will also be impeded by various people who persist in taking an unbalanced view of the existing state of affairs and of where we are going. Optimists will select those features in which real progress has been made and, laying stress on these and ignoring other features, will proclaim that 'All is for the best in the best of all possible worlds', and pessimists will point to those features where evil still prevails and will proclaim loudly that our efforts are leading nowhere. 'Vanity of vanities', they will say, 'all is vanity' (Ecclesiastes i, 2).

But despite all difficulties, obstacles and misrepresentations we shall gradually come to accept the guidance of God, to work in harmony with him and to distinguish his voice from that of Satan. We know that Christ is always with us (Matthew xxviii, 20) and that if we, as an army, fight the good fight valiantly with Christ as our Commander, we shall slowly but surely build the kingdom of God on earth. We know also that in so doing we shall gradually bring Satan to realise that defeat is certain. His attacks will become less powerful, and although he will no doubt from time to time rally and launch a vicious attack in some unexpected quarter, we shall learn how to repel or even to forestall it and our victory will ultimately be achieved. We shall then dwell in this earthly realm with Christ as our leader for an indefinite period. During this period, when Christ will be supreme on earth, we shall be undergoing further training to fit us for the final stage of our journey to salvation. This period of training on earth will, however, come to an end, for the earth cannot last for ever. The final stage of our journey, both as individuals and for the human race collectively, will also be the consummation of our service to God, and will take place in eternity where, when God decides that we are ready for the supreme mark of his approval, our temporal life will be raised to eternal life.

Since the conditions that will prevail in God's kingdom are fully known only to God, we must always be ready to admit, while building the kingdom, that our vision may be impaired and that Christ alone, and not our fallible wisdom, must be our guide. Nevertheless, there are some features of the kingdom of God that have already been revealed to us, or of which we may, by our experience, be reasonably certain, and also some initial steps that must obviously be taken if we are to avoid disasters so great that the fulfilment of our task will be indefinitely delayed.

We know, for example, that in the kingdom of God we shall not be entirely free from sin. Even after the defeat of Satan and his repentance, when our struggle against him will have been brought to a successful conclusion, we shall still be imperfect and will fall from grace from time to time. We may expect, however, that as we build the kingdom of God we shall come to understand the problem of sin and evil more fully and will gradually eliminate the errors inherent in our present outlook (see pages 113–120).

We know also that the two basic principles of competition and interdependence, which God has introduced into his created universe to guide its evolution and inform all its manifestations, and which we have so damagingly disturbed, will be brought more nearly into balance so that by co-operation between them progress in the right direction may be assured. As an offshoot from this the dominance of economics (the worship of Mammon), a consequence of our reliance on increasing the production of wealth as a means of remedying all the world's ills, will be subdued, and new economic systems, more nearly in accord with the teachings of Christ, will be developed (see pages 125-29).

Our belief that all technological advances are beneficial and are inspired (or even ordained) by God and should therefore be promoted and encouraged will also be discarded, and means will be devised to subject them to prolonged and detailed scrutiny by those who, because of their unworldly lifestyle, may be held to be competent to advise on whether they should be adopted and developed (see pages 129-35).

The most significant change from our present outlook will be the gradual realisation that the true objective, the objective that will bring the greatest satisfaction, is not the pursuit of happiness, which sometimes has evil origins, but the joy that will come from unity with and in Christ and the knowledge that we are doing the will of God. Happiness will not be lost, for it is good, provided that the circumstances in which we find happiness are good, but it is not the greatest good; it will, as we build the kingdom of God, be subsumed in joy, which has its roots in eternity.

An Analogy

In our efforts to understand the development of the human race towards the fulfilment of its assigned destiny, it is helpful to compare this process with the development taking place in the life of a human being. We can also relate it to the allegorical accounts of the origin and the early stages of humankind as given in the first few chapters of Genesis. We do not know when human life, characterised by the possession of a soul, was first created, but it is probable, if not absolutely certain, that the earliest men and women were unaware that they were *essentially* different from all other animal species. However, the course of history shows that in due time they came to understand, or at least to feel, that they were linked, in some explicable way, with a Being or beings of a higher order than themselves. This stage of development, which may have lasted several thousand years, corresponds with the nine months which the human embryo and foetus spends in its mother's womb, during which time, after its soul has been created and implanted, it learns spiritually, though of course not intellectually, that it is linked to God by the bond of obligation and is thereby enabled, at a later stage, to grasp the concept of duty.

For many thousands of years men and women remained, from God's point of view, in a state of infancy, dependent on his bounty for their sustenance, as an infant depends on its mother (or another person) not only for its food but for being fed. Moreover, as a newborn infant is innocent, so also the earliest men and women were innocent, not knowing the distinction between right and wrong. Nevertheless, the knowledge, however hazy, that they were linked to God and were therefore essentially different from all other created beings on earth was critical, as an infant's first realisation that it is essentially different from a family pet or a cow or sheep is critical for its future development.

Satan is of course always ready to pounce, but although an infant quickly learns about its immediate surroundings the content of its mind is at first too small to provide Satan with adequate material on which to exercise his wiles. Nevertheless he is not idle, and will seize the first opportunity to attack the growing child's mind, with the object of corrupting its soul. So also the early members of the human race, giving intellect pre-eminence over instinct, gradually accumulated knowledge of the world around them, and at the same time learned from God the distinction between right and wrong. Satan immediately took advantage of this; he set about confusing their minds, persuading them that what God had told them was right was really wrong, and vice versa. This whole period of human development is described allegorically in the second and third chapters of Genesis as the Garden of Eden. Adam and Eve were at first innocent (not knowing that they were naked). They were not aware of sin; in fact they had no knowledge that in creating them God had a purpose, so that sin, which is the failure to adopt that purpose as a guide to thought, action and development, could be intelligible to them. However, in due course God implanted in their minds the concepts of right and wrong by telling them that they could eat the fruit of every tree in the garden except that of the tree which stood in the centre of the garden, the tree of the knowledge of good and evil, concepts which at that stage of their development would have been too difficult for them to understand. Of course this provided Satan with the opportunity for which he was waiting. He seized on it, persuading Adam and Eve that what God had told them was ridiculous; that so far from suffering any damage by eating the forbidden fruit, they would gain enormously, becoming like gods. This initial success of our enemy has hampered our efforts to defeat Satan throughout the whole of history, but should not lead to despair, for we know that our ultimate victory is certain.

Later the human race entered on the period corresponding to early childhood. In Genesis this period is symbolically represented by Cain and Abel. During this period, also lasting many thousands of years, intelligence developed enormously, though at first very slowly. Men and women began to learn that they had the power to control and augment God's bounty and to bend it to their wishes; they learned to till the soil (Cain) and to domesticate animals (Abel). They acquired many other skills as their childhood stage advanced.

Although the early chapters of Genesis are clearly allegorical and not to be taken as a scientific account of the evolution of life on earth and of the creation of the human race, it is remarkable how closely the allegory fits the facts. As an example of this parallelism we may point to the fact that the earliest men and women were, like their immediate primate ancestors, almost certainly entirely herbivorous, but at some later stage, possibly some thousands of years later, became carnivorous. It is true that some primates today are carnivorous, but we do not know when God decided to create the human race by implanting souls in a selected group of primates, or indeed what precisely this selected group was. It is therefore not unreasonable to assume that it was herbivorous. If we make this assumption, the facts tally exactly with the biblical account. Adam and Eve were allowed to eat herbs and fruit (Genesis i, 29; ii, 16); permission to eat meat was not granted until after the Flood (Genesis ix, 3, 4). This phrase should be interpreted simply as 'some time later', for we do not know when the Flood occurred or even whether it occurred at all; if it did it was probably a purely local affair.

As a child learns that his own desires are not the only determinant of action, that there are rules to be obeyed and prohibitions to be observed, and that over and above those imposed by his parents there are laws and obligations imposed by a higher authority, so also human beings, in the course of their evolution, gradually learned that, in spite of their great powers and their superiority to the inanimate world and to other forms of life, they were not the highest form of being. There were gods, or a single divine being, whose powers were greater than theirs, and who, they came to believe, in some ways and to some extent controlled their destiny. Moreover, as a child may try to bribe an adult to allow it to breach a rule or to avoid a punishment, so also the human race adopted the practice of offering sacrifices to their god or gods in order to appease them. As they could not see these more august beings or speak directly to them, they made icons and other images whereby some of their essence could be expressed and even revealed; and they also made songs in their honour. In this way the concept of art, music and poetry, as media for revealing the essence of God, developed.

With the onset of adolescence the child begins to discard the restraints which he has hitherto accepted as an inescapable part of the circumstances of life. He then becomes adventurous and rebels against authority, often with very damaging consequences. The human race entered on this stage of adolescence about two and a half centuries ago, and during the present century its rebelliousness has been virtually uncontrolled. The consequences will be very painful, but as an adolescent grows to maturity and begins to learn that conformity with the law and with the rules and conventions of society is not a restriction on liberty but an essential requirement of social cohesion, so also the human race will cast aside the follies of the present age and will begin to grow in the wisdom that can be acquired only by complete submission to the will of God. We shall not, however, accept this discipline easily; we shall learn to do so only by coming to realise that the calamities that must now inevitably befall us during the coming century are the inevitable consequences of our present foolish and hubristic assumption that we can rely on our unaided judgment for the kind of society that we wish to bequeath to posterity.

Evil and Sin

It is always salutary to admit ignorance, and we are especially called upon to do so in these latter days in which our minds are overwhelmed by the advances made in science and technology. We are tempted to look back on those who lived in earlier centuries and to pity them for their lack of so many skills, devices and techniques that are available to us. We have come to believe that we have now reached a state of sophistication that will lead to further triumphs and enable us to create a utopia on earth. This belief is, of course, false, and in no sphere is our ignorance more profound and baffling than in the mysteries of evil, sin and suffering. We may, however, confidently expect that, after we have overcome the catastrophes into which our present follies must inevitably lead us (see pages 98–100 and 103–4) and have made some progress in building the kingdom of God on earth, we shall be given further enlightenment on these mysteries; but for the time being the most that can be attempted is an analysis of some of the factors involved.

For this purpose we must return to a consideration of the action taken by God in the Creation. The successive stages of this stupendous task have been described in Chapter 2, but as an introduction to the analysis of the problems posed by the existence of evil, sin and suffering in the world, it will be convenient to summarise them here.

In the Nicene Creed we proclaim that 'we believe in God the Father Almighty, maker of heaven and earth and of all things visible and invisible'. In this we acknowledge that the whole of creation is the handiwork of God, whose being is supra-eternal. Eternity proceeds from him (page 28), and he created the angels, giving them eternal being and eternal life. They dwell in eternity and are co-eternal with God. He created the physical universe of space and time, matter and energy, endowing it with temporal being, and ordained the laws governing its evolution. He created temporal life and implanted it in the universe, so that plants, fish, birds and animals appeared in due order and evolved in accordance with his laws. He created mind, and at the appropriate time added this to the equipment of certain living species, thus associating the physical and psychical universes. And finally, he created the souls of human beings, to dwell like the angels in eternity, thereby linking eternity with time. He endowed all human souls with eternal being and temporal life, and also with wills whereby they could exercise freedom to determine their own evolution, albeit subject to certain restraints.

From this all-inclusive statement it can be argued that God, being the Creator, is responsible for everything that has happened, and everything that will happen, in time, including all the evil in the world. But in God there can be no evil; to say otherwise would be a contradiction in terms. For the meaning of 'evil' is 'falling short of the essence of God', and God cannot fall short of his own essence. There is an apparent contradiction here, which needs to be resolved. The problem is not new; it has always been with us. It is sometimes presented as a question: 'If God is omnipotent (as most theistic religions claim) why does he allow evil to flourish in the world?' or 'Why does suffering so often fall on the innocent rather than on the guilty?' These questions have been asked in every generation and will continue to be asked for many years to come. A partial answer has been given by earlier theologians, in particular by St Thomas Aquinas, and this will in time be amplified as the human race grows in maturity and wisdom. The clearer understanding thus obtained will then percolate through the whole of the world until the existence of evil ceases to be a problem.

We are told that when God had finished the work of creation (including the creation of human beings) he looked on everything that he had made and saw that it was very good (Genesis i, 31). But it was not perfect, for God alone, the fount and origin of love (agape), is perfect. The created world is therefore imperfect, but it is not evil. Evil enters only where there is sin, and sin involves the wrongful exercise of free will. It follows that nothing in the inanimate world, or in the living world apart from the human race, can be evil in itself, even though it is imperfect. The earth on which we live is unstable and the weather is largely unpredictable; earthquakes, floods, hurricanes and forest fires occur and may cause great damage and great distress and loss of life, but they are not evil. The verse from Genesis quoted above shows that when men and women were first created they also were not evil. They were, of course, imperfect but they had no knowledge of sin, as the embryo or foetus in the womb is innocent of sin. Their first task was to learn that they were linked to God and their second task was to learn how to co-ordinate this link with their obvious connection with, and reliance on, the world around them. It was this stage that gave Satan an opportunity to pervert their minds and souls, thereby tempting them to sin. They did not wholly resist the temptation; they allowed themselves to be misled, and thereby sin entered the world

In speaking of evil and sin it is very important to be quite clear about the meanings of these words. They are, in fact, often misused, and this not only causes confusion but will certainly impair our judgment. If we say that something is evil, we are attributing a characteristic to it. We have, of course, no right to attribute this characteristic to anything that God has made; if there is evil in anything it is because we have ourselves corrupted God's handiwork. We ought indeed to be careful, if we describe anything as evil, not to imply that in it there is no trace or element of good, for we are not entitled to suggest that anything lies beyond God's redemptive power.

The word 'sin', whether used as a noun or a verb, and the adjective 'sinful', are applicable only to eternal beings, and therefore on earth only to human beings. They are not merely epithets describing a characteristic of a person, they imply a relationship between that person and God. Sin is a disease or malfunctioning of the soul. It involves partial alienation from God and a partial blocking of the channel of obligation by which the soul is linked to God. Thus the word 'sin' implies belief in the existence of God and of a relationship binding God to the sinner. Sin is an impairment of this relationship. We should avoid coupling the word 'sin' with the word 'against', for such coupling suggests that we can sin against another human being or against an animal or against nature, leaving God out of the picture. Carrying this false linguistic usage to an extreme, we might even say that it is possible to sin against Satan, for he is as much a creature of God as any human being. We ought not even to speak of sinning against God, for this is tautological, and failure to recognise the tautology impairs our judgment.

This is an important point. For if we make no linguistic distinction between an offence against God and an offence against one or more of his creatures, we are easily led to eliminate the distinction between God, the supra-eternal Being who is the source, the *fons et origo*, of the concepts of goodness and of duty, and his creatures, especially his human creatures, to whom the first of these concepts is being revealed and on whom the second is imposed. The error of failing to make this distinction is insidious and the risk of falling into it is ever present. The risk is enhanced by the fact that the two categories so largely overlap; an offence against any of God's creatures, especially his human creatures, is in many or even in most cases also an offence against God. Naturally, Satan takes full advantage of this by encouraging the misuse of language. Even the evangelist Matthew was not immune. For in chapter xviii of his gospel he uses the word *hamartias* (sin) in two places (verses 15 and 21) in reference to an offence committed against a fellow human being ('my brother', 'thy brother'). It must, however, be borne in mind that he was recording, in Greek and long after the event, words probably spoken in Aramaic; also that, like all human beings, he was fallible. In recording the Lord's Prayer (chapter vi) he was more careful (see page 120).

Wrongful thoughts, words and deeds are normally the products of a disordered mind. The disorder may be momentary, as when we suddenly lose our temper, or it may be chronic, as when someone deliberately adopts a life of crime. In almost all people these two types of disorder are present, but in different proportions. The causes of the mental disorders which give rise to wrongdoing are partly genetic and partly environmental, but these are not the only or even the most potent causes. The attitude of the soul, the extent to which it is in accord with or in conflict with the will of God, though indirect, is also important and in the long run may, without our being fully aware of it, be the most potent factor in the determination of action. For the soul can, and does, use the genetic and environmental features available to it and fosters or suppresses them in accordance with its own determinations.

If we see or hear of a wrongful act we are likely to say that the perpetrator has committed a sin. It would be impossible to alter this linguistic usage but we should recognise that it is careless and even hubristic, for we are not in a position to judge the degree of sinfulness in the soul of the wrongdoer. It is probable that any breach of the Ten Commandments, or of the wider commandment 'thou shalt love thy neighbour as thyself', whether by thought, word or deed, involves a sin. It is, however, possible that when a person is to outward appearance behaving very badly, his soul may be striving valiantly to overcome and eliminate the defects of character, both bodily and mental, which led to his behaviour, and which may in large part have their origin in genetic factors or in a distorted ethical code attributable to the environment in which he has been brought up or into which he has been thrust by circumstances beyond his control. He may be very wicked, but in his inmost being, his eternal being, be striving to improve. In such a case God judges, not by what he is, but by what he is striving to become. We cannot judge the state of anyone's soul by his outward behaviour. We should bear in mind the words spoken by God to Samuel when he was seeking to discover, from among the sons of Jesse, who should succeed Saul as king of Israel. Six times God rejected Samuel's choice, saying 'The Lord does not see as men see, for men see only appearances, but the Lord sees into the heart' (1 Samuel xvi, 7). Again, when David was telling his courtiers that the temple would not be built by him but by his son, he turned to Solomon and said 'And you, my son Solomon, acknowledge the God of your father, and serve him with whole-hearted devotion and with a willing mind, for the Lord searches all hearts and discerns whatever plan may be devised' (1 Chronicles xxviii, 9). And Solomon in his prayer of thanksgiving after the temple had been built, said 'Thou alone knowest the hearts of all men' (Kings viii, 39). The fact is that we are not competent to judge the state of another's soul, for God alone is the judge of sin. This is emphasised by Paul, who asks 'why dost thou judge thy brother?' and reminds us that 'we shall all stand before the judgment seat of Christ ... every one of us shall give account of himself to God'. He follows this reminder with the plea 'Let us not therefore judge one another any more; but judge this rather, that no man put a stumbling block or an occasion to fall in his brother's way' (Romans xiv, 10–13). And finally, we have the command of Christ: Judge not, that ye be not judged' (Matthew vii, 1).

We are not even able to assess accurately the degree of our own sinfulness. We may know when we do wrong, and it is certainly salutary to confess our wrongdoing and to resolve to correct our defects of character. We should also try to remedy any damage to others to which these defects may have contributed. But we have lost touch with our own souls and cannot judge their sinfulness, which finds expression not only in action but also in the extent to which we have contributed to the false objectives of the human race as a whole, and therefore also to the moral confusion and the distortion of moral values which are such prominent features of the present age.

In fact, the most potentially harmful sins are not the sins of individuals but communal sins, the sins of the whole human race, or of some large and influential part of it. In the case of a communal sin, the sin may not be present in the soul of every individual in the group, but it must be supported by a sufficiently large part of it to be able to produce a climate of opinion in which nearly all the individual members may be engulfed. The consequences of a communal sin are far greater than the sum of the consequences of the presence of that sin in the souls of the members of the group. This has always been the case, but it is particularly true of the communal sin of the Western world at the present time, because the Western world, by virtue of the vast increase in knowledge which it has acquired during the past two or three centuries, is able to influence the thought of humankind as a whole. These sins consist, for the most part, in the adoption of false beliefs, tampering with God's laws, particularly with his evolutionary laws, and generally pursuing false objectives, prompted by Satan, thereby creating a moral climate and conditions of life in which individuals are subjected to new temptations, which they do not recognise as such, conditions in which they are often unable to distinguish right from wrong. We can well imagine what joy the creation of these conditions brings to Satan's heart. But by succumbing to these temptations individuals commit actions which in a purer moral climate would spring from the sinful soul of the individual, but which God in his mercy will recognise as being due more to communal sin than to the sins of the individuals concerned. Many of the social evils which are so prominent today – e.g. marital breakdown, the rise in crime and drug abuse, and the disregard for authority among the young (in breach of the Fifth Commandment) – will not be laid at the door of those committing the wrongful actions involved in these evils, but will lead rather, by the inexorable operation of God's laws, to the punishment of the whole community. As we allow Christ to enter our souls and build God's kingdom we may hope and confidently believe that the influence of communal sin, at present overpowering, will diminish towards vanishing, thereby giving rise to conditions in which Christ's statement 'By their fruits ye shall know them' (Matthew vii, 20) will be given its true validity.

In support of the contention made in the above paragraphs that the word 'sin' means 'an offence against God', and ought not to be used except to describe a relationship with God, we may note that, in teaching his disciples how to pray (Matthew vi, 9–13; Luke xiv, 1–4), Christ did not say 'Forgive us our sins as we forgive those who sin against us'. In the version quoted by Matthew there is no reference to sin; in both cases the word he used was *opheilma*, which means debt. Luke rightly distinguishes between an offence against God and an offence against another human being; his version is 'forgive us our sins [*hamartias*] as we forgive those who are indebted to us'. In both Matthew and Luke the meaning to be attached to the word 'debt' is not limited to the repayment of a monetary loan, it covers any failure to discharge a duty, of whatever kind, which we owe to God, to another person or to other people.

Although the ability and the right to assess the measure of sin are reserved to God alone, we are entitled to applaud or condemn the actions of others as we think that they contribute or are inimical to the well-being of humankind as a whole, and to mete out rewards or penalties accordingly. It is right to condemn obvious wrongdoing and to take appropriate steps, by punishment or otherwise, to prevent wrong-doers from repeating their offences. If punishment is inflicted it should, as far as possible, be designed to reform the offender, but the objectives of protecting the public and of reassuring the victims of crime that their sufferings have not been forgotten or overlooked and will so far as possible be relieved must be given equal importance. The desire for revenge should, however, be totally absent from the minds, not only of those who are charged with the duty of inflicting the punishment and those who pass the laws prescribing what punishment or other remedial action is appropriate, but also from the minds of the public at large (cf. Deuteronomy xxxii, 35; Romans xii, 19).

Suffering

The problem of suffering is as baffling as that of sin and evil, and its solution, in so far as we can understand it, is also to be found in the fact that, although God is omnipotent, he cannot refrain from expressing his own essence. He created the angels to be the active recipients of his love, and he endowed them with the power to respond to it and with the freedom to determine the measure of their response. He knew that, being imperfect, the angels would not respond fully and that in the case of some the response would be very weak. He knew also that the defect of their response would cause him suffering, as all unrequited love causes suffering. Thus suffering is an inevitable consequence of the fact that God is love.

We can, however, go further. God knew not only that the response of all angels would be incomplete, but that some would reject his love entirely and would rebel. Moreover, he knew that this rebellion, in addition to increasing his own suffering, would infect eternity with a 'spiritual virus' whereby it became diseased. Eternity has therefore become, as a result of Satan's defection, a medium in which suffering is transmitted from one eternal being to another. Satan has actually damaged an emanation proceeding from God himself, and it will be part of our duty, after the defeat of Satan, and all (or nearly all) human beings have attained to eternal life, to remedy the effects of the malicious organisms which Satan has implanted in eternity and restore it to health.

When God created the physical and psychical universes, he knew that suffering would inevitably become a feature of them. For Satan, having discovered how to damage eternity, would certainly apply the same technique to time and space. Naturally, he took advantage of the fact that pain and discomfort are necessary in the higher animal species in order to secure their survival, and when human beings were created with power to determine their own evolution he was overjoyed. Knowing that the capacity to experience pleasure and the capacity to experience pain are closely related, he encouraged people to develop the former to the maximum. The consequence is that in the human race the experience of pain is far greater than is necessary for the preservation of the individual or of the species. Having accomplished this evil feat, he exploited it by working on the desire inherent in most people to dominate their fellow human beings (see pages 79–80), corrupting this desire into a desire to inflict cruelty, with results that are recorded through the whole of history (see pages 82–83) and are even more evident today. It will be part of our task to reverse these trends when we start to build the kingdom of God on earth.

There are many references to the wrath of God in the Bible, many passages in which he is depicted as vengeful, calling down plagues, famines and other disasters on humankind as punishment for their sinfulness. The prophet Ezekiel even likens God to a school bully, threatening punishments on Moab, Egypt, Edom, Tyre, Sidon and other cities and nations, and ending each threat with the words 'Then they will know that I am the Lord'.

These accounts, arising from the error of anthropomorphism, of reducing God to human level, the error which leads to our misuse of the word 'sin', convey a false impression. The sinfulness of humankind undoubtedly causes suffering to God and inevitably also causes suffering to men and women, 'even unto the third and fourth generation'. This suffering is the inescapable consequence of the laws of the physical and psychical universes which were ordained by God, not as a means of venting his wrath, but because they are an essential part of his plan for the defeat and redemption of Satan. We must accept these facts and endure the sufferings they entail, and we must believe that as we receive Christ and build God's kingdom, these same laws will reduce the incidence of suffering in the world.

The Moral Code

There is an absolute moral code. It is necessary to state this emphatically because at the present time it is denied by many people. There are even a few people who deny that a moral code of any kind exists; that the words 'moral code' are meaningless. They would argue that all behaviour is governed by heredity and environment (thus denying the existence of free will), or that no restrictions should be placed on the exercise of free will other than those imposed by the law of the land in which they live.

This extreme position is, however, rare. The majority of people who deny the existence of an absolute moral code do not entirely reject the idea of a code; in other words, they admit the existence of a higher authority than that of human law. Their position is that the moral code is dependent on circumstances, that what is right at one time or place may be wrong at another, or that what is right for one person may be wrong for another. This position is obviously not wholly false; indeed, it contains a great measure of truth. Error creeps in, however, if those who take up their stance on the fact that the requirements of the moral code vary according to the circumstances, or are unclear, use this as the basis of an argument for denying the existence of an absolute code.

There is such a code. It is the code which everyone would feel obliged to follow if original sin, which is the communal pursuit of false objectives, had not led to the creation of circumstances in which strict adherence to the precepts of the absolute code has become impossible, or in which certainty about what its precepts enjoin is unattainable.

If the absolute code had been complied with unreservedly from the moment when the human race was created, Satan would have been wise to admit defeat from that moment. Of course he would not have done so; he would have continued to launch his attacks against an impregnable fortress, his rage against God would have continually increased and he would have adopted a new strategy to attain his ends. We do not know what this would be but we may hazard a guess that he would have tried to destroy the universe which God had created. This, of course, is no more than speculation on the circumstances of an impossible situation. It is not, however, idle speculation, for it serves the purpose of focusing attention on the reason for this impossibility. This is that, as human beings are created, they are necessarily imperfect and have therefore always been incapable of strict compliance with the absolute moral code.

All this was known to God in advance. He knew that the nature of the task that human beings were created to fulfil could only be revealed to them gradually, that Satan must be worn down slowly and that they must be allowed to evolve in order that they should be equipped, by learning from their mistakes, to meet Satan's changing tactics. This situation is still with us. In fact, the problem has become more acute. For with the increasing scope of our intellectual compass Satan has found it possible to aim his weapons at new targets and to introduce even greater confusion than ever before into our understanding of right and wrong.

God has always known that full compliance with the absolute code is beyond our reach, but he requires that we shall so mould and guide our evolution that we shall create conditions in which knowledge of the absolute code becomes easier to attain and compliance with it more nearly within our power. In the meantime, he allows a contingent code, less stringent than the absolute code, to be the guide for our daily lives, and he requires that we shall continually ask him to reveal to us the precepts enjoined by this contingent code. We have some knowledge of these precepts: we know that they fall short of, and in some instances may even be incompatible with, those of the absolute code, but we do not know how much latitude is allowed to us. We ought, of course, always to fix our sights on the Ten Commandments and the teachings of Christ, knowing that they point the way. But as we have already seen in Chapter 1 (pages 4–7 and 9), these have at all times left many questions unanswered, and the complexities of modern life have enormously increased the grounds for confusion on moral issues. Scientific and technological advances have raised new problems and have added their quota to this confusion. Euthanasia, abortion, divorce, the portrayal of violence and sex on television, the protection of minorities against the encroachment on their freedom and their rights occasioned by acceding to the will of a majority – these and many other moral problems are the subject of daily dispute. On all these the requirements of the absolute code, if they were known, would be unattainable in our present state of immaturity, and our knowledge of what is obligatory and what is permissible under the contingent code is obscure in detail and far from complete.

In these circumstances our duties are twofold. Both duties require us to seek continually and to resolve to accept the guidance of God, and this requirement can only be met by our keeping open, in defiance of Satan, the channel of obligation linking us to God, allowing the Holy Spirit to cleanse it and inviting Christ to enter our souls. The first duty is to discover what is allowed and what is prohibited under the contingent code applicable to the circumstances of today, and the second is to mould our future development in such a way that the contingent code may be brought, slowly but surely, into coincidence with the absolute code. We shall not embark fully on this second duty until we have passed through and overcome the calamities into which our present and past follies will lead us, but our ultimate success is certain.

Economics

The basic principles on which the laws governing the development of living creatures on earth are founded are competition and interdependence (see pages 14–15). God has so balanced these apparently conflicting principles that they co-operate in harmony to control evolution in accordance with his plan, and if disharmony occurs it is because we have disturbed this balance. We do not know whether these two principles govern the evolution of the angels in heaven or of living beings in other parts of the universe, and this knowledge is not necessary for us at the present time. It is, however, necessary that we should accept God's dispensation on earth as a guide in formulating the principles on which to build human institutions, and this is of particular importance in the sphere of economics. For our decision to accept the theory, prompted by Satan, that salvation is attainable by the unlimited increase in the production of wealth has led to the dominance of economics in all activities of our lives. From this it follows that, if our system of economics is faulty, our lives will be less satisfactory than they need to be, to God as well as to ourselves, and the system itself is liable to suffer from disease.

These two divine principles inhere in human nature, as in all God's creation, and they are readily seen in the two economic theories, capitalism and communism, which have dominated the conduct of the world's affairs in the twentieth century, though in a distorted and unbalanced form. Communism has tried to rely exclusively on interdependence, ignoring the naturally competitive element in human nature, with the result that, in those countries where it has been the accepted economic system, interdependence has ceased to be voluntary and has been rigorously imposed by a tyrannical authority. Because of this imbalance, it is collapsing and is unlikely to survive for long in the coming century. Under capitalism, on the other hand, the stress is laid on competition, interdependence being invoked only when it serves the interests of competition. This system is also unbalanced and is bound to collapse within a few years. Many signs of its inevitable demise are indeed already visible.

Both these systems have served their purpose and must be allowed to die. To take their place we need a new economic system and an economist of the stature of Adam Smith or Karl Marx to formulate and promulgate it. We cannot rely on the normal processes of economic development under the pressure of events to bring this new system into being. A new underlying theory is required. For circumstances will continue to change and there must be a generally agreed doctrine to provide a basis on which the measures needed to meet those changing circumstances can be debated and put into action. Without this doctrinal basis the measures taken will be merely pragmatic, and in the harsh circumstances that will follow the breakdown of the present systems the outcome of economic pragmatism unsustained by doctrine can only be chaos. In economics as in religion, doctrine is an essential framework without which the working rules for the application of the system to the problems of daily life will be the subject of endless controversy, and the system will break down.

The details of these rules must be worked out by specialists, but if the new economic system is to have the power of endurance in the changing circumstances that will emerge as we begin to win the war against Satan, it must embody four principles.

The first principle is that, in order to avoid conflict with God's dispensation, the system must ensure that competition and interdependence are properly balanced. And since the economist (or economists) responsible for formulating the new system will be largely influenced by the prevailing culture, the opinions of the general public on the conduct of affairs must also be guided by this principle.

The second principle is that the new system must, in its dealings with living beings, whether vegetable or animal, and with the soil whence they derive their sustenance, cease to put a premium on efficiency. Efficiency, in the sense of obtaining the greatest return from the material available, is a valuable principle when the material under consideration is non-living (e.g. the world's mineral resources), but when it is applied to living matter it is already proving to have dire consequences and must inevitably, in the perhaps not very distant future, lead to disaster. In particular, if it is applied to human labour, disguised as productivity, it promotes an attitude of mind in which men and women are, in this respect, equated with machines, and this is not only degrading to human beings and an insult to God, but also has undesirable practical consequences that may be more readily understood in a secular world. For the replacement of men by mechanical or electronic devices, if not controlled by appeal to a higher law than that which encourages the creation of wealth as the highest good, must lead either to increasing unemployment or to increasing pressure to develop and maintain new markets for highly technical equipment, thereby divorcing men and women even more widely from their roots in nature. From this it can be deduced that the new economic system must incorporate a means of reducing, even to vanishing point, the dependence of the price of goods and services on the number of people employed in producing or providing them. And, of course, this must be done without reducing the real remuneration of the producers. It is impossible at present to suggest how this can be done, and it might even be held that the problem is insoluble, since any solution would seem to contravene the laws of arithmetic. But the mind of man has overcome greater difficulties than this, and it would be both unwise and defeatist to assign any limit to human ingenuity where, as in this case, the need is imperative. Since we must never, in any circumstances, however threatening, relinquish the belief that man has a future, we may be certain that this problem, like so many seemingly insoluble problems in the past, will not prove to be beyond the power of our inventive genius.

The third principle, no less important and no less immediate than the first and second, is that the new system must take account of the culture and ideals of the peoples of the Third World as well as of those of the Western and Eastern blocs. Capitalism is the product of the mind of Western man, which, being based on a scientific approach to both physical and metaphysical problems, has become increasingly materialistic with the passage of time. Communism has claimed to have a more idealistic foundation, but its rejection of God has led, in practice, to its adopting even more materialistic goals and forcibly imposing them on the peoples of those countries whose economies it governs.

Hitherto we have, in our dealings with the Third World, either compelled or tempted the people to accept those materialistic values, which have great seductive power. But as Christians, we know very well that, although we readily succumb to them, they are not ultimate values (Matthew vi, 19–34), nor are they such as can be imposed on peoples of non-European origin without doing grave psychological and even spiritual damage. So the new economist must, in constructing his system, ensure that it does not give rise to conflict within the minds of those for whom scientific materialism is not a natural reaction to the problems of reality, and especially the problem of understanding the true function of humankind.

The fourth principle is not concerned with objectives but with structure. It is that the system must be, and be seen to be, self-policing; in other words, it must be so devised that those who infringe, disregard or try to undermine its rules, or to take improper advantage of them, should, by virtue of the mechanisms embodied in and the procedures based on those rules, suffer retribution. And this must not only follow swiftly on the wrongful action but also be readily seen to be the inevitable consequence of that action, and not ascribable to other causes. Capitalism has evaded this principle by the provision of facilities for loans and credit, subject to interest charges, and in communist states it does not apply at all, since the controls are not inherent in the system (though Marxist theory would require this) but are imposed by authority, more often on political than on economic grounds. The new system must therefore be devised in such a way that, to the greatest extent possible, those who are tempted to abuse it will be deterred, not by the fear of punishment by an external authority, but by the operation of the system itself.

Of these four principles the first is the most fundamental, and from it an important deduction may be made. This is that, while we must hope that the new economic system will serve humankind for at least half a millennium, it must be framed with a more distant end in view. Its authors must believe that their efforts are directed towards the realisation of the ultimate destiny of humankind. When viewed in this light it is easily seen that it will not suffice to devise a system that is sufficiently flexible to deal with immediate difficulties, such as unemployment in the year 2000 or a shortage of certain types of skilled labour in 2020. It must, of course, take these difficulties in its stride, but it must also be so framed that those who are entrusted with its administration can clearly see that the solution to these immediate problems is of little moment in comparison with the grand design, formulated by God before the beginning of time, to bring harmony into every part of his creation.

Science and Technology

The errors of regarding science as a panacea and of promoting the uncontrolled growth of technology, and the disastrous consequences to which these errors will inevitably give rise, have been pointed out on pages 86–87. Only direct intervention by God can avert the calamities that are now portending (see pages 98–100), and although we may be certain that he will intervene to prevent the annihilation of the whole human race by a nuclear war (page 100), we cannot expect him to intervene to avert those consequences of our folly that fall short of universal suicide. For in the war against Satan our training as an army can only be achieved by our learning from our mistakes (see pages 67 and 98). We know therefore that the mistakes we have made will be the cause of much suffering and that this will continue until we have acquired sufficient wisdom to lead us to change our outlook and our priorities, in short to repent (*metanoein*). We should also pray unceasingly that God in his mercy will ameliorate the calamities and the suffering, that they may be no greater than is absolutely necessary to bring about our repentance.

There are also practical steps to be taken which must not be delayed. The most pressing of these is to dismantle all nuclear power stations. All human artefacts are imperfect, and accidents at atomic power stations are therefore inevitable. Alternative sources of energy must be urgently sought which are renewable for as long as the human race is likely to survive on earth, and at present it would seem that the only such sources are the sun and tides. Objections will at once be raised, pointing out that these have been examined and found to be impractible or too expensive, but all such objections should be overridden. A group of dedicated scientists should be appointed with instructions to solve the problems and to report within five years. In the meantime, coal-fired power stations should be restored, and another group of scientists appointed to find means of collecting the effluents of such stations and rendering them innocuous before releasing them.

Obviously, these changes will require international action,

and steps should be taken immediately to establish an international authority, armed with drastic enforcement powers as well as with powers to acquire territory for experimental purposes and to direct the activities of the scientists engaged in the task of developing safe sources of energy. As an example, the international authority might take possession of the Sahara and other deserts and cover them with solar panels, selling the energy so produced to those countries which are unable to provide safe energy from their own resources.

Although the dismantling of all atomic power stations and the safe disposal of the fuel rods and other equipment used in them is the most urgent task in this field, it is not the only one. Many other scientific and technological activities need to be brought under strict control if we are to minimise the social as well as the ecological damage caused by our present greed and folly. The replacement of human beings by computers, with the consequent rise in unemployment and crime, the increase in stress-related psychological disorders and the fracturing of personal relationships, must be, if not halted, at least retarded. Stricter controls are also desirable over virtual reality, the Internet and possibly also films and television programmes. Above all, the freedom at present exercised by scientists to conduct genetic experiments must be curtailed. An accident or an error in this field might have disastrous consequences lasting many thousands of years.

Here again international action is called for, but a start must be made somewhere, and the United Kingdom, with its unique constitution, is well equipped to make this start. A Ministry for Posterity should be established, charged with the duty of scrutinising every large-scale technological advance and deciding on its probable effect on humanity over a period of not less than 250 years. The ministry should be given power to prohibit entirely, or to prohibit except under licence, the commercial exploitation of any technological development or any course of scientific inquiry which it considers may be detrimental to the well-being of posterity. For the purposes of enforcement the ministry will need only a small number of Civil Servants to implement its decisions and to take remedial or punitive action when these are infringed.

The Minister will, however, need advice of a kind that Civil Servants cannot give. For this purpose a permanent committee should be appointed and, bearing in mind that theology is still the queen of the sciences, even though it is no longer regarded as such, this committee should contain a strong theological element. It should contain senior representatives of all the Christian denominations, of Judaism, Islam and Buddhism, and possibly other religions. It should also contain a philosopher, a representative of the arts, a historian and a lawyer, each eminent in his or her faculty, and representatives of the relevant sciences – physics, chemistry, biology, psychology and ecology. A total of about twenty members should suffice, and no member should have a vested interest in any matter brought to the committee's consideration. The chairman of the committee should be the Minister, and the Permanent Secretary of the ministry should be its vice-chairman. The committee should have power to summon witnesses and to examine them on oath, and its decisions should be binding on the Cabinet.

These measures will be opposed on the ground that they curtail freedom. To this objection, however, three answers can be given. The first is that all law limits the freedom of the individual in the interests of the well-being of the community, and in this instance the damage to the community that will result if the law is not enacted as proposed is so great that draconian measures are justified. The second ground is that the establishment of a Ministry for Posterity in the United Kingdom is only an initial step. It can only be effective if this initiative is followed by other nations, and if the enactments passed are consolidated into international law and administered by an international authority. Once this has been done, provision can be made for those who feel that their liberty has been wrongly curtailed by a decision of the Ministry for Posterity to have a right of appeal to the international authority.

The third ground is theological. Briefly, it is that the restrictions imposed will be only temporary, although 'temporary' here may mean several hundred years. The establishment of a Ministry for Posterity is required because we have allowed

Satan to mislead us into adopting a way of life which, if not amended, will go far towards destroying the earth that God has created to be our habitation while we are engaged in the task assigned to us for the fulfilment of his purpose. We shall, however, be brought to repent, to realign our wills to accord more nearly with the will of God, and thereby to make a start on building God's kingdom on earth. This will necessarily be a slow process, lasting perhaps several thousand years, but gradually more and more people will allow the Holy Spirit to cleanse their link with God and allow Christ to enter their souls and guide the further evolution of the human race. As this process advances, the restraints imposed by the Ministry for Posterity will gradually be lifted.

In a well-known prayer we ask God to give us the strength and courage to change those things which ought to be and can be changed, the serenity to leave untouched those things which cannot be changed and the wisdom to know the difference.

In its application to individuals the meaning of the prayer is clear enough. We can, and sometimes ought, to change our characters. We can, within limits, even change the influence of our genetic structure, and we can, within very narrow limits, control our environment by choosing our friends or our job, but we cannot, except marginally, change the general environment in which we conduct our lives, otherwise than by fleeing from it, e.g. by entering a monastery or a convent, an option that is open to very few.

The real significance of the prayer lies in its communal application, and here we have done some strange things. We have, particularly in recent years, tended to ignore the second category completely; indeed, we have hardly been aware of its existence. Nevertheless, it is a very important category, for it includes many of the basic truths of Christianity, and indeed of all religions. In particular it includes recognition of the unique mode of the existence of God (supra-eternal being); the fact that he is three Persons; the manifestation of existence at two lower levels (eternal being and temporal being); the laws implanted by God in the universe to govern its evolution; the power of the individual will to mould character and of the communal will to direct the course of human evolution; the existence of angels and in particular of malevolent angels under the command of Satan; the fact that God has created us for the specific purpose of waging war on Satan and defeating him, thereby bringing him to repentance and redemption; and the facts that Christ, by his death and resurrection, has partially disarmed Satan, thereby ensuring our ultimate victory and eliminating the prospect of the death of the human race and of all its members, which would be the inevitable consequence of our defeat – also that he is willing and eager to lead us in the battle, to ignore our shortcomings and to help us to overcome them, if we will allow him to do so by admitting the Holy Spirit to enter and cleanse the channel of obligation linking us to God. And finally this category includes the fact that by the power of prayer we can enlist God's help in all difficulties and dangers and that this will be freely given, provided that our prayers are sincere and in accordance with his will.

Although we have ignored the second category, we have not left ourselves without choice. For we have taken into account the fact that there is a third category, the category of those things that can be, but ought not to be, changed. Obviously, the distinction between the first and third categories should be maintained, for they require different treatment. But in this we have signally failed. We have obliterated the distinction and have merged the two categories by discarding the concept of 'ought' or 'duty', thereby rendering the prayer vacuous and impairing our relationship with God. For duty is an essential part of that relationship; the word 'duty' can only be defined by reference to the fact that God has a purpose and that we are included among the agents chosen by him to bring that purpose to fruition. We are charged with the duty of changing those things that ought to be changed and of refraining from changing those things that ought not to be changed, but we have assumed that we have a right to change anything that can be changed if we believe that it is in our interest to do so. We are therefore rewording the prayer; we are asking God to give us the strength and courage to change what can be changed if that is what will, in our view, promote our interests best; we are in effect saying: 'Let our will, not thine be done' (cf. page 105).

Clearly we must restore the word 'ought' to the prayer and order our lives accordingly. And for this we shall need wisdom. For our present attitude has led to the commission of many follies, and of these some of the most dangerous have been related to our efforts to alter the tempo of the laws of the universe as ordained by God. Thus climatic changes have taken place throughout the whole of the earth's history, but they have taken place very slowly, over periods of tens of thousands of years, but we, by polluting the atmosphere, have brought about global climatic changes which may in due course have a devastating effect and may delay the conquest of Satan indefinitely. God designed the laws of biological evolution to operate very slowly, but we have tried to accelerate them by an enormous factor by genetic engineering. We are allowing the computer to become our master, as we have allowed the internal-combustion engine to become our master, and the former is injuring our mental health as the latter is injuring our physical health. One of our most recent follies has been that of compelling cattle, which God in his evolutionary plan has created to be herbivores, to become carnivorous, with disastrous consequences.

By deleting the word 'ought' from the prayer, we are committing the sin of hubris, of rating our judgment above the guidance of God. We must therefore restore the distinction between the first and third categories, and we must also restore our recognition of the existence of the second category and of what it contains – the things that cannot be changed – for without this knowledge we cannot effectively accomplish the purpose for which we have been created. Full understanding of the three categories and of our rightful behaviour in relation to them requires wisdom, and in the prayer we rightly ask God for this gift. For wisdom is not attainable by human effort alone. As Solomon has taught us (1 Kings iii, 5–12), it is a gift from God, which he readily grants if we seek it by constant and universal prayer. There is no point in looking to science or other sources of knowledge to provide it, although increased knowledge may well be an important factor; above all, we must not hope to find the seed of wisdom by genetic research, for there is no gene for wisdom.

Restraints

Since our souls dwell in eternity and also in time and space, and are a link between these two media, and since the eternal order has dominion over the temporal order, the powers residing in our souls are immense. We know that they have power to choose their objectives and to secure the achievement of those objectives by creating, annihilating and modifying desires, beliefs, emotions and other psychical attributes, thereby creating our individual characters and, over several generations, moulding our evolution. It is by exercising this power that we determine our strategy in the war against Satan; for this reason it is free and unconstrained, and is probably also free of all restraint by God.

This, however, is not the only power possessed by our souls. They have many other latent powers, and in so far as the exercise of these powers involves overriding the laws of the temporal order, they are performing miracles. It is only to be expected, therefore, that, so long as the human race is immature and unable to distinguish clearly between good and evil, or even between right and wrong, because of Satan's extraordinary histrionic abilities, God should impose restraints on the exercise of the soul's thaumaturgic powers. By the same reasoning we may expect that, as we grow in maturity and become more familiar with Satan's tactics and more able to resist them and to treat them with contempt, some of the restraints will gradually be lifted and we shall rejoice in greatly enhanced freedom. Three examples of this greater freedom are relevant to the theme of this book.

First, the power of an individual soul to communicate directly with a kindred soul, which is a constituent of agape, will be greatly increased. It already exists, although in the present confused state of our minds and souls it is seldom understood or even recognised. It is almost certainly an element in the relationship between two people who are genuinely in love, but because in such cases agape (a condition of the soul) and eros (a condition of the mind and body) are both active, the confusion is almost impossible to resolve.

The lifting of this restraint will probably take place in two stages, of which the second will be divided into four substages. In the first stage the power to communicate telepathically will become more widespread and more reliable. Telepathy is a means of communication between mind and mind, but the soul of the initiator can instruct the mind over which it has control to transmit a message to another mind. This, however, is an unsatisfactory means of spiritual communication, for the soul of the recipient is free to accept or reject the message presented to it. The use of telepathic powers is at present very limited, but that is not to say that they do not exist. It has already been suggested (pages 42–43, 47) that some plants and animals possess telepathic powers, and it would be remarkable if human beings did not also possess them. But whereas plants and animals are not free and can only exercise their telepathic powers in accordance with God's ordained laws, human beings are free, and in so far as they allow their wills to be guided by Satan rather than by Christ, they will certainly misuse these powers. For this reason they are at present held in restraint by God, but as the war with Satan begins to show real results and we are thereby encouraged to wage it more vigorously, the restraint will gradually be lifted.

In the second stage a much more powerful means of communication will be made available to us. In this stage soul will communicate directly with soul, through a medium which has its being in eternity, without using the mind as an intermediary. This will increase the speed of evolution in accordance with God's will and will therefore also promote the building of his kingdom. In the first substage of this development direct spiritual communication will be reserved to people who have an affinity with and who know one another; in the second substage this will be extended to people sharing a common language and seeking allies in the promotion of a particular line of development. The third substage will be marked by a new manifestation of our latent powers, in that the range of communication will be worldwide and will take place without the use of language; spiritual ideas being comprehensible by the souls of the people who have nothing in common save a mutual desire for a fuller understanding of God and of his purpose for humankind. In the fourth and final substage this will be extended to embrace the whole universe.

The second function of the soul which is now severely restrained and is relevant to the purpose for which the human race was (and is still being) created is the power to perform healing miracles, to remedy defective limbs and organs and restore them to their full strength, to cure diseases, both physical and psychological and, in very rare cases, to raise the dead to life.

It is recorded that these powers were used by Elijah and Elisha (see pages 93-4) and possibly other prophets, and Jesus, who performed many healing miracles, conferred them on his disciples and instructed them to use them (Matthew x, 1; Mark vi, 13; Luke ix, 1, 2). After the Resurrection miraculous cures by the apostles Peter and Philip are recorded in Acts iii, 1-11; viii, 5-8; and ix, 32-34; and we are told (in Acts ix, 36-42) that Peter raised Tabitha to life. Paul also performed similar miracles (Acts xiv, 6-10; xx, 9-12; and xxviii, 7-10). However, it is obvious from the story of Ananias and Sapphira (Acts v, 1-11) and Paul's reproof of the Corinthians (1 Corinthians v) that the early Christian communities allowed themselves to be subjected to very severe discipline, and were therefore unlikely to misuse their miraculous healing powers. Later, as the Christian community grew and was more widely spread, control within it became more difficult and therefore less strict. The risk residing in the power to heal miraculously, a power which could be used to inflict disease as well as to cure it, increased, and accordingly this power was placed under increasingly strict control, though never entirely withdrawn. Origen (*c.* 185-254) tells us that the gift of healing by the Holy Spirit was customary until the end of the second century but then became very rare. Nevertheless, it is probable that this gift is still available to a few people, but these are more likely to be found among 'primitive' people than in 'advanced' countries where the power of the Holy Spirit is inhibited by the psychological disorders and the moral confusion that are so characteristic of the Western world. Whether in advanced or in primitive countries, however, the gift of miraculous healing is not to be sought among the most powerful, the most learned, the most intelligent or the most artistically gifted people. The criterion applied by the Holy Spirit is whether the individual soul is willing to open the channel of obligation, which is its link with God, and allow the Holy Spirit to cleanse it. And, since humility before God is an essential step towards admitting the Holy Spirit, we can recognise the aptness of Mary's prophetic claim that 'he hath put down the mighty from their seat and hath exalted the humble and meek' (Luke i, 52).

The facilities available and the skills displayed by physicians, surgeons, pathologists, psychiatrists, nurses and paramedics are now truly amazing and awe-inspiring, and ought also to inspire in us gratitude to God for his benevolence. But these facilities and skills are very unevenly distributed and there are many millions of people who do not now enjoy them and are unlikely ever to do so. For already, even in the most 'advanced' countries, the provision of health care is showing signs of strain as demand begins to outstrip supply and economic factors inhibit expansion. And this imbalance is certain to get worse as the demand for health services increases. This increase will be due in part to the expectation of the less developed countries of the world to share in the advantages available to those who live in countries where hospitals are adequate to meet the needs of the population and are equipped with all the most advanced scientific appliances; but many other factors will contribute to the imbalance between supply and demand. Among these we may cite the increase in world population (about 100 million a year at present); the increasing proportion of old people in the population; the pollution of the atmosphere, giving rise to increased pulmonary disorders; the unpredictable consequences of damage to the environment in other ways; the mutation of pathogenic organisms to become resistant to medical treatment formerly successful, and further mutations resulting from accidents in genetic research; the increase in the incidence of cancer and other diseases that will result from accidents at nuclear power stations which, as already pointed out (page 100), are certain to occur; and the incidence of psychological disorders which will inevitably result from our reliance on electronic devices in the conduct of our lives, both in the office and at home.

This discrepancy between supply and demand in the provision of facilities for health care would be likely to continue and increase for at least two centuries if it were not forestalled by the calamities that must inevitably ensue from our present disordered outlook, but at the same time the inequality between the advanced and the less developed countries would be gradually ironed out. After these calamities have been overcome and by submission to God's will, we will begin to build his kingdom on earth. The provision of remedial facilities for those who are sick or injured or diseased that can be made by orthodox medicine based on scientific principles will be slowly supplemented by miraculous healing. It must be recognised, however, that the role of miraculous healing must always be limited. There are two reasons for this. The first is that only a few people will be allowed to use this power, and the second is that it cannot be effective unless both the healer and the sick person have complete and unadulterated faith in the process. This last point is made abundantly clear in the accounts of miraculous healing given in the New Testament. In many cases Jesus said to the person seeking his help 'your faith has made you whole' (see, for example, Matthew ix, 22), and both Matthew and Mark record that in his home town (Nazareth) he 'did not many mighty works there because of their unbelief' (Matthew xiii, 58; Mark vi, 5, 6; see also Matthew xvii, 14–21). Further, although Jesus cured a few people without touching them or even being close to them, it is questionable, and I think unlikely, that human beings will be able to exercise their powers in this way. For both these reasons they will be unable to use their healing powers to deal with plagues or epidemics.

Thus, so long as there are human beings on earth, miraculous healing will not entirely replace medical treatment based on scientific research. But the latter will be increasingly subject to control as public opinion becomes more fully governed by the knowledge that the usurpation and use of powers which God wills should be exercised by him alone will inevitably lead to disaster. The power of miraculous healing, and also the power of spiritual communication (and possibly other powers at present being restrained by God) will, on the other hand, be developed during our time on earth, as these will be needed after death before we attain to eternal life. For, as we have already seen (page 90), at the moment of death the substance of the body is transformed into mental substance, and the body and mind thus united will be given eternal being, as they are raised to the ontological status of the soul. Our souls, therefore, though still differing in substance from our bodies and minds, will have even greater power to control the development of individual character and the course of evolution than during our earthly life. Our bodies and minds will, however, still be imperfect and will be subject to psychological diseases, and our souls will still be capable of falling into sin. For this reason the gift of eternal life, whereby complete freedom from restraint will be conferred on body, mind and soul, will be withheld until we have undergone further training. During this period both the power of spiritual communication and the power of miraculous healing will be needed since physical means of communication and healing will not be available. And as our training proceeds and we become more Christlike, these and possibly other powers will be given greater freedom.

The third faculty of the soul which is relevant to the future of humankind and is at present either latent or non-existent is the power to control fertility miraculously – that is to say, by the direct action of the soul on the body. This faculty is closely allied to the power of miraculous healing but is an example of the soul working in the opposite direction. For in the case of miraculous healing, the soul acts to restore normality to an abnormal condition; in the case of fertility control, the soul acts to ensure that the result of sexual intercourse will be abnormal. This, however, is not to be interpreted as meaning that such action by the soul is wrong; on the contrary, it will certainly be contingently right when it becomes possible and may even be absolutely right. Indeed, the exercise of this power will become increasingly important as we build the kingdom of God on earth.

The manner in which this power will be used and the choice of those who will be permitted and empowered to use it must be to some extent a matter of speculation, but the need for it is clear enough. For it is becoming increasingly evident that the world cannot accommodate its present population (5.8 billion) without ecological damage which may prove to be irreparable, and both physical and psychological disorders which will detract from the quality of life.

For thousands of years before the beginning of the twentieth century the population of the world remained below two billion. It had grown slowly since the creation of humankind, reaching one billion by about 1830. It had been maintained at a fairly steady but very slow growth by the operation of natural law. People may have had large families but many children died before reaching maturity. God tolerated this means of ensuring that the world population would remain steady, but his tolerance was clearly a temporary expedient, for it is abundantly clear that he wills that everyone should live a healthy life. This is attested by the fact that Jesus spent much of his time in healing the sick and crippled.

Since the middle of the nineteenth century medical science has made enormous strides, with the result that, in advanced countries, infant and child mortality has been reduced to a level that is probably not far above the minimum possible. Disease has, of course, not been abolished, since we all must die, but diseases affecting children and adolescents have largely been replaced by those of middle age and old age, with the result that the expectation of life at birth is now higher than at any previous time in human history. Even in less developed countries the birth rate is at a level that ensures a continual growth in population.

It is probable that the maximum population that the earth can support without irreparable damage to the environment is about 3.5 billion. It is also probable that world population will be reduced to about this figure by the ecological, economic and social catastrophes that will occur during the twenty-first century, probably starting before 2050. Thereafter the state of society will be very unstable for perhaps two hundred years, as philosophers, theologians, politicians and other leaders of thought seek means of stabilising society and directing it to submit to the will of God. During this time natural law, supplemented by artificial methods of contraception, will maintain a fairly steady level of world population. There will, of course, be fluctuations, but any signs of a runaway increase in population will lead to restrictive measures imposed by social pressures.

It is, I think, certain that artificial contraception will be needed for many hundreds of years; it will be opposed by the Roman Catholic Church and possibly other religious bodies, but this opposition will be overruled by the growing realisation that the preservation of the earth that God has provided to be our habitation must take precedence over all other considerations. As the world advances in spirituality, God will confer power on selected people to control their fertility by the direct action of their souls on their bodies, miraculously determining whether any act of intercourse shall be fertile or not. This power will be limited to those who satisfy him that they will allow the determinations of their souls to be guided by the Holy Spirit. They are likely, at first, to be few, but will in due course cover the majority of the population of the world.

I have assumed throughout this section, particularly in regard to spiritual communication and miraculous healing, that our souls already possess powers which are not visibly apparent because they are latent and held in restraint by God. It must be mentioned, however, that there is an alternative theory, namely that our souls do not actually possess these powers, but only the capacity to receive them as a gift of the Holy Spirit. This theory would seem to be the one favoured by

Origen in the passage quoted above (pages 138–39). Indeed, Origen goes further; his words imply that it is not our souls that perform miracles of healing when so empowered by the Holy Spirit, but the Holy Spirit who performs the miracles, using the souls of human beings as a channel. Paul also recognises that it is by the power of the Holy Spirit that human beings perform miracles, at any rate those miracles that are pleasing to God (for we must not forget that in the formation of our characters and in directing the course of human evolution we perform many miracles that are *not* pleasing to God); but he does not suggest that we play no active part, although he states that the decision on who shall be selected to receive particular miraculous gifts rests with the Holy Spirit (1 Corinthians xii, 7–12; also Romans xii, 4–8).

These distinctions are fine, but consideration of them is not mere quibbling, for the answer to them is relevant to our understanding of our relationship to God and the extent to which he has entrusted to us the responsibility for the conduct of the war against Satan. We know that he will not intervene, without our asking him to do so, in a manner that would curtail our freedom. He will intervene in answer to prayer which accords with his will, and he has of course intervened by being incarnated in Jesus Christ. Apart from this supreme intervention when, after the Crucifixion, he descended into hell and limited Satan's power by depriving him of eternal life without impairing our freedom, we know that he does not and cannot overtly take the initiative in directing the course of events in which human beings are concerned. We know this, not only for the reasons given on pages 24-25, but also because it is attested by all experience. It is also borne out by the fact that we must be free to make mistakes, since it is by learning from these that we become effective soldiers in God's army. Where human beings are not involved, God is, of course, in complete control, though only indirectly, through the operation of the natural laws by which the universe is governed. Satan is well aware of this and makes no attempt to attack those laws; on the contrary, he makes use of them by persuading men and women to pervert them to serve his purposes. On every occasion when he is successful in this, he is causing human beings to use their thaumaturgic powers to defeat God's purpose, and our defence is to invite the Holy Spirit to cleanse the channel of obligation which links us to God and to allow Christ to guide us in the use of all our powers, including the power to work miracles, and to extend those powers when we can be trusted to use them rightly. We must hold fast to the certainty that, in spite of our present difficulties, this happy outcome will in due course be achieved.

5

The End and the Beginning

The immensity of the universe is a feature of God's handiwork that cannot be ignored. It inspired awe in the Psalmist, who proclaimed exultantly that the heavens declare God's glory (Psalm xix, 1). It also inspired him with humility (Psalm viii, 3, 4). We know that everything that God has done is essential to the fulfilment of his purpose and that, as his agents, it is our duty, so far as lies within our finite power, to discover the reason for and the meaning of every product of God's handiwork. We are therefore impelled to ask why God has found it necessary to create a universe so large and complex. It is possible that the complete answer to this question is summed up in the Psalmist's response – to inspire us with awe and humility and to give us some insight into the majesty of the infinite God. This is certainly part of the answer, but I cannot believe that it is the whole answer, and I think it probable that this doubt is shared by most people who have given thought to the matter.

It is much more likely that God knew, before time and space were created, that the wiliness and power of Satan is so great that he could not be defeated by one race of free beings alone. it is probable that, as suggested on pages 64–65, we, the human race on earth, are engaged in battle with only one, or possibly a small number, of Satan's lieutenants, and that in other parts of the universe other creatures, resembling us in that they have both eternal and temporal being but otherwise perhaps very different, are engaged in warfare with other agents of our common enemy. If this is true, it may also be true that God has found it necessary to be incarnated many times and in many parts of the universe, to give guidance to the soldiers fighting there and to assure them of their ultimate victory.

On earth the path to victory will be opened when we have overcome the calamities that must ensue from our present state of rebellion. We shall then learn to pray for wisdom and for the humility whereby we may allow Christ to be the captain of our souls, by asking the Holy Spirit to cleanse the channel of obligation linking us to God. When our war, and those of all other soldiers in God's armies throughout the universe, have finally been won, possibly many thousands of years in the future, and all Satan's lieutenants have been defeated, the final onslaught on Satan himself will begin. It will be very different from our local warfare against his lieutenants, for Satan will then put forth all his powers to avoid defeat. In waging this final onslaught on Satan we shall be in spiritual communication with our companions throughout the universe and will wage war as one army under Christ's leadership. We shall discard our defensive attitude (pages 69–70) and will take the offensive, rejoicing in the knowledge that victory is close at hand. In this final battle we shall use only one weapon: the power of divine love, which will be ours to use and which we and our companions from other parts of the universe will have in our possession, because Christ will have, at our request, put himself in charge of our souls. Against this weapon Satan will be powerless; he will be defeated and will receive back the seed of eternal life which had been lost when Christ descended into hell after the Crucifixion. He will be required to cleanse this seed by repentance (*metanoia*) of all the evil with which he had polluted the universe. This will be a very painful task, but we and all our fellow soldiers, who will have been rewarded with the gift of eternal life, will be glad to help him and his lieutenants towards their redemption.

This will be the end. But it will also be the beginning, for we will then be required to enter on our service to God in heaven, and this will continue throughout eternity. We may be certain that God has a further task (or tasks) for us (and for our other-world companions) after Satan has been defeated and we have attained eternal life. We do not know in detail what these tasks will be, though it is possible, or even probable, that in accordance with John xvi, 13 they will, at least in part, be revealed to us while we are still engaged in our war with Satan. We can, of course, speculate, and it is our duty to do so, for in this matter, as in all matters concerning our relation to God, the responsibility rests on us to seek to discover his purpose and constantly to ask by prayer for his aid in revealing the nature of our task in the fulfilment of that purpose, so enabling us to discharge that task to his satisfaction. This is a salient characteristic of our relationship with God. He does not, and will not, compel us to accept and to do his will, nor will he forcibly inject into our understanding all the details of his purpose. As I have repeatedly stated in this book, he does not interfere with our freedom unless it becomes necessary to do so in order to ensure that his purpose is not frustrated. As in the case of the angels (page 23), a compelled response is valueless to him and would only retard our training. God will always respond generously to a sincere request by us, provided that it accords with his will, to the extent that our souls, minds and bodies are ready to receive his guidance, but we must take the initiative.

Before inquiring into the nature of the tasks God will require us to perform in heaven, we must consider the circumstances of our personal life there. In this voyage of exploration we shall be entering largely uncharted territory and we must proceed with caution. But we cannot shirk the obligation, for it is here that lies hidden the riddle of God's ultimate purpose for those whom he has created in his image. We may be certain that in due course we shall solve this riddle and that all secrets that concern our duty to God will be revealed. But we do not start from a position of complete ignorance, for in the endeavour to learn what God has in store for us there are a few certainties on which we can build our beliefs and our expectations.

First, each of us will be aware of his or her own identity. For our essence lies in our souls, and every soul of every human being has been and will be created individually. Every soul will in heaven be accompanied by, and will have at its disposal, those bodily and mental faculties which it has created or has retained and fostered from the bodily and mental material at its disposal during earthly life as being most fully in accord with its own chosen objectives. All these, the soul and its objectives, and the bodily and mental faculties accompanying the soul, will have undergone the cleansing process of Purgatory before being accorded the gift of eternal life. Every individual soul will have spiritual substance, its bodily and mental faculties will have mental substance and all will have eternal being and eternal life.

Every human being will, therefore, be ontologically very nearly on an equal footing with Christ, who at his resurrection retained, though with spiritual substance, the physical and mental characteristics which he had possessed during his lifetime on earth, thereby enabling him to act effectively as our advocate with his Father. We shall be the sons and daughters of God the Father, differing from Christ only in that he is begotten of the Father whereas we shall be his children by adoption and grace.

Secondly, it will be noted that in the two preceding paragraphs I have assumed that, although there will be no marriage in heaven (Matthew xxii, 30), the distinction between male and female will be preserved and will endure throughout eternity. This fact is vouched for by the account given in Genesis of the creation of man. We are told (Genesis i, 27) that he created human beings male and female, and this can only relate to the creation of their souls, because the bodily (and in part the mental) distinction between male and female had already taken place in the ancestors of the human race by the forces of evolution.

The laws of evolution were laid down by God at the beginning of time, and the fact that they were devised to give rise to two sexes is evidence that this distinction is part of his plan, which required a difference of body and mind to provide suitable housing for the two distinct types of soul while engaged on their tasks on earth. In creating the new priorities and in devising and establishing the new social institutions required for building the kingdom of God on earth, the female soul and the female mind will play a much greater and more significant role than has hitherto been the case.

We may expect that the complementary principles of competition and interdependence will prevail in heaven as they do among living creatures on earth (page 14). They will co-exist as guiding principles in every soul, but the predominant principle will in male souls be competition and in female souls interdependence. The degree of predominance will differ between one soul and another, and God will assign specific tasks to suit the balance prevailing in each soul. There will be affinity between the sexes and it is probable that individual male and female souls will tend to pair together in such a way that each pair produces an even balance between competition and interdependence. Male and female souls will rejoice in co-operating to do God's work. Neither sex will dominate the other; indeed the idea of domination over others, which is the source of so much suffering on earth (see page 79), will be entirely absent. Dominance will be accorded to God alone.

The third point in our consideration of the circumstances of our life in heaven is that our souls will not find it easy to adapt themselves to the greater freedom they will be able to exercise in heaven; they will also have difficulty in learning how to take on the new responsibilities imposed on them. Every soul, of course, dwells in eternity from the moment of its creation but at first enjoys only temporal life, in which it is unable to explore eternity freely and thereby to obtain full knowledge of God's purpose for all his spiritual creatures. When our souls attain to eternal life this restriction will be lifted.

With the limitations imposed by our temporal life (which we must remember continues in nearly all cases for some time after earthly death) we find it difficult to comprehend eternity. A fuller understanding will be available to us after we attain to eternal life, although it will probably not be revealed to us in a flash but will be acquired gradually. This suggests that there is a link between eternity and time, and instinctively we feel that this is the case, although we cannot define precisely the nature of that link. Our understanding is confused, and the confusion is enhanced by the fact that, in the New Testament, the Greek word *aionios* is sometimes translated 'eternal' (as in Matthew xix, 16) and sometimes 'everlasting' (as in Matthew xix, 20). We know that eternity is not endless time and that eternity and time are in fact quite distinct, since eternity streams out unceasingly from God (page 27) and is therefore part of his essence, whereas time is created.

We can, however, gain an inkling into the relation between time and eternity by picturing eternity as a multi-dimensional medium and time as a moving point tracing out a line in that medium. The line as it now exists comprises the whole of the past, and each point of the line comprises all the events that occurred throughout the whole universe at the moment in time represented by that point.

When we consider the fact that time and space were created to provide the conditions necessary for the creation, in due course, of human beings (and possibly other free beings) charged with the duty of defeating Satan, it might be thought that, once that purpose was accomplished, time and space, having served their purpose, would be annihilated. If this supposition is true then time will ultimately have an end; the moving point in eternity will cease to move and the line it has traced out will not be further prolonged. This is the assumption I have made earlier in this book (pages 2, 31–2, 46) but we cannot be certain that it is correct. God may have some further purpose to be carried out in time (with or without its companion space), in which case the moving point will continue to trace out the line in eternity indefinitely, and in what follows I shall assume that this will be the case.

The concept of a moving point in a multi-dimensional medium is, of course, only an analogy, but it serves the useful purpose of enabling us to define the greater freedom which our souls will acquire when the gift of eternal life replaces temporal life.

Our knowledge of the past is fragmentary. It consists of our memories of experiences in our own lives, including our contacts with other people and with the outside world, and of what we have been told or have read or imagined, and have believed to be true, about events falling outside our own direct experience. Such knowledge is, of course, incomplete and may be inaccurate – our memories are fallible – and in regard to past events in which we have not ourselves played any part, either directly or by observation, it is notorious that different historians will give widely differing accounts. We can in part repair these deficiencies by asking questions of those whom we believe to be knowledgeable and by further study, but such repair is only partial, and so long as we are bound to time, even though dwelling in eternity, we cannot attain to the degree of knowledge of the past that will be necessary to enable us to discharge the tasks that God has in store for us.

When we attain to eternal life we shall, of course, be able to communicate with those who have taken part in any particular past event. This communication will not be through a physical medium, as communication is on earth, but by telepathy and spiritual communication (see pages 136–38); but although we may by these means be able to increase vastly our knowledge of the past, it will still fall far short of what God may require of us. For it will still be only human knowledge, whereas what God requires is knowledge of him and of his will. Of course, in regard to any particular event in the past God has complete knowledge of the minds and souls of every participant in that event and its preceding causes, and this knowledge is encapsulated in the point in the line of time in which that event occurred. In eternal life our souls, perhaps after a period of training, will be able to travel through eternity to different points in the line of time, and will do so in accordance with God's instructions. We shall be able to enter into any point, not, of course, to modify anything that it contains (for the past cannot be altered), but to observe it as fully as may be necessary to discover God's reactions to every part of that event as it unfolds. And this knowledge is important, for our duty in heaven will be, as it is on earth, to seek to know God more and more. We cannot know him completely, but we must, and in heaven we shall, seek to know him as far as our finite souls and minds allow. For it is only thus that we shall be able to discharge the tasks that God has assigned to us in the fulfilment of his unending purpose.

Paul has hinted at these facts in the first letter to the Corinthians, where he says: 'for now we see through a glass, darkly; but then face to face; now I know in part, but then shall I know even as also I am known' (1 Corinthians xiii, 12). Paul was speaking personally, but his words apply to events in times past generally as much as to the personal life of each member of the human race.

Our bodies and our minds will also face a difficult task in adapting themselves to the circumstances of eternal life and the functions they will have to exercise and the duties they will have to perform in that life. Our bodies having discarded their physical substance, will no longer need food and drink to preserve themselves, nor will sexual intercourse be necessary to preserve the human species, although as already stated the distinction between the sexes is retained. What will remain and will be preserved will be those cerebral faculties whereby our bodies are able to feed our minds with information about the universe that God has created, including, of course, the people living in it.

Our bodies will, however, not have to face the conditions prevailing in heaven without preparation, for they take on their transformed state at the moment of earthly death and, (except in the case of Mary, the mother of Jesus) do not enter into eternal life until later. The length of this interim period is not predictable; it is decided by God, who, knowing all the relevant circumstances, will assign the moment of its termination.

The difficulties that our minds will have to confront will be greater. For in addition to having to absorb the experiences which our souls wish to pass on to them from their own expanded freedom, they will then have to learn how the minds of the angels work, so that they can communicate effectively with them. This at once raises a problem. If, as described in Chapter 2, the psychological universe was not created until after Satan's expulsion from heaven, the angels, who are co-eternal with God, must have been created without minds. How, then, can we be called upon to communicate with them mentally?

The answer to this question is complex, and carries with it

an interesting implication. It is almost certain that the angels, as originally created, did not possess minds. They did not need them; they were spiritual beings whose sole duties were to understand God and to respond to his love, both of which were (and are) spiritual activities. (We also have these duties and they are carried out by our souls.) There was no external universe, the understanding of which would involve mental activity. Even after the creation of the universe but before the creation of the human race, the angels had no function to perform in regard to the universe, and had no need of minds.

The whole situation changed with the creation of the human race. When mind was first implanted in the more highly developed animals (and possibly also in a very limited way in all animals and even in the vegetable world) its activities were restricted to those necessary or favourable to the preservation of the individual and of the species, and the progress of evolution in accordance with God's plan. It acted as a storehouse for such information as was necessary for these purposes, as an organ capable of experiencing emotions and as an activator of life-preserving instincts. Contact with the world of the angels was unnecessary. Mind acted as an agent of the telos, which used it to discharge the role for which it was created; neither mind nor the telos aspired to any higher role.

The human mind, however, as described in Chapter 2, is not thus limited. Moreover, human beings have a moral sense which, like their minds, is independent of the telos and cannot be explained by reference to enlightened self-interest. They can grasp the concepts of purpose and duty, they have access to the spiritual world and are linked to God by the bond of obligation. Their minds must be able to receive information and instruction from their souls and are therefore endowed with an additional dimension through which spiritual messages can be delivered. God further decided that in these processes the 'good' angels, those who have responded positively to his love, should play a part; he therefore endowed them also with this further dimension of mind, the dimension which was added when the human race was created. These angels were required to use this to assist in communication between the spiritual world and the human world and thus became, as their name implies, messengers between God and humankind.

This raises the question whether particular angels are assigned to guide and assist particular human beings, in other words whether the concept of guardian angels is valid. Many people believe in guardian angels, although the scriptural authority for such belief is scanty. The best-known texts on which to base the belief are the promise given to the Israelites on their journey from Egypt to Canaan 'behold, I send an angel before thee, to keep thee in the way, and to bring thee into the place which I have prepared' (Exodus xxiii, 20), and that from which Satan quoted in his second temptation of Jesus: 'there shall no evil befall thee, neither shall any plague come nigh thy dwelling. For he shall give his angels charge over thee, to keep thee in all thy ways. They shall bear thee up in thy hands, lest thou dash thy foot against a stone' (Psalm xci, 10–12).

It remains to consider what will be the fate of those other angels, the 'bad' angels, whose response to God's love is negative, some of whom may even be on the point of rebelling against the 'good' angels and against God. Among these, strife and envy, dissent and quarrelling, jealousy and malice, disregard of rules and rejection of authority, are prevailing characteristics (as they are on earth at the present time), and as a consequence God regards them as being unfit to be the guardian angels of or messengers to humankind. Obviously, these must be brought to see the errors of their ways and in due course to obtain redemption through repentance. For God's ultimate purpose must be to reign over a heaven in which harmony will prevail, strife will have been brought to an end, and all created beings will seek to know and to do his will.

In this task Michael and other archangels have been engaged throughout the whole of eternity, but it has proved to be beyond their power. When Satan rebelled they made war on him and were able to expel him from heaven, but they could not bring him to repentance. War may then have been necessary to avoid the spread of Satan's corruption to other angels, but it is not by aggressive war* that they can be brought to repentance. And in this there is an obvious lesson for us here on earth.

The service we shall have to render to God in heaven now becomes obvious. It will be to act, no longer as his soldiers but as his apostles, in aiding Michael and other 'good' angels in the task of bringing the 'bad' angels to repentance and redemption. This task will be never-ending and from time to time there will be relapses, both on our part and that of the angels we shall be trying to help, but progress towards success will continue throughout eternity.

The weapons we shall use throughout our apostleship will be agapeic love and the power that this confers. Our efforts will be directed to convincing the angels that Christ's death on the Cross embraced their redemption as well as ours, and that his resurrection was a guarantee of ultimate success in leading them towards that redemption. This task will not be easy, but we shall be well equipped to cope with it. We shall, of course, dwell alongside the angels in eternity and will resemble them in having eternal being and eternal life, but will nevertheless be very different from them. From being a little lower than the angels (Psalm viii, 5) we shall have been raised to be their superiors and their mentors. For we shall be ontologically more complex than they are, possessing bodies (albeit of mental substance) as well as souls and wills, which the angels certainly possess. We shall also have minds, which at first the 'bad' angels do not possess, but which they will need to enable them to respond effectively to our teaching. It is probable, therefore, that our souls, which have creative power in the mental field, will be required to create minds in selected angels who are progressing towards repentance, and we shall call upon these to assist us in fulfilling God's unending purpose. In our efforts to bring about this consummation we shall have an enormous advantage over the angels by reason of the fact that we shall actually have defeated Satan and brought him to

---

*See pages 69–70.

repentance. Without going into detail, Paul hints at this ultimate destiny of humankind when he says to the Corinthians 'Know ye not that we shall judge angels?' (1 Corinthians vi, 3).

The final, but not the least important, point to be made in this (admittedly incomplete) description of our life in heaven is that the ideal experience at which we shall aim, and by which our efforts to serve God will be rewarded, will not be pleasure or even happiness, but joy. On earth quite trivial (and sometimes even harmful) events can bring about a state of happiness, but happiness can also be experienced by uplifting causes which lead to closer contact with, or greater understanding of, God. The joy which we shall experience in heaven will be akin to the happiness which springs from such uplifting causes, but will be a deeper emotion, having spiritual as well as mental content. The trivial or harmful causes of earthly happiness will, of course, be repudiated and will be wholly ineffectual in heaven.

On earth we can approach the heavenly experience of joy through great art (including sculpture and architecture), great literature and great music, in the production of which the writers, artists, composers and executants are striving, possibly unconsciously, to fulfil their true role, which is to reveal the essence of God. On earth art, whether true or false, usually requires some physical medium to provide the experience, but certain people can visualise an artistic production or hear a musical composition in their imaginations, and this experience of true art, literature or music will certainly be available to some people, possibly to all, as part of their life in heaven.

The inspiration provided by the Muses will, of course, not be the only source of our joy. Prominent among the other sources will be the friendships and intimate relationships we shall form with other human beings and other created beings of our own time and of earlier and later times, and with the angels, including those who will be acting as our partners and those who will be our pupils and whom we shall be leading to repentance. Over and above these relationships will be our growing friendship with Christ, who, without actually taking part in our work of teaching and reforming recalcitrant angels, will give us all the help we need and ask for. He will also bring us, slowly but unceasingly, to a fuller knowledge of God the Father, an end which on earth is sought not only by the path of mysticism but also by that of prayer, and which ought to be the true objective of all philosophers and theologians.

The conclusions we reach from the analysis set out in this book may be summarised as follows:

(1) that God's love, which is his essence, is outgoing and requires living beings to receive it;

(2) that these beings are the angels, from whom God demands a free response to his love;

(3) that God, being the creator and demanding a free response, has authority and can require, though he does not compel, obedience to his will;

(4) that these facts are resented by some angels, who rebel and cause disharmony in heaven;

(5) that throughout all eternity God has had a purpose, which is to restore harmony in heaven;

(6) that we human beings have an essential part to play in the unfolding of that purpose;

(7) that in order to enable us to fulfil that role we have been endowed with souls and wills that have eternal being and are therefore free and unconstrained by God, though they are subject to certain restraints which will be partially lifted as we progress;

(8) that the freedom of our souls and the fact that they have been created to serve God's purpose impose on us duties, and that the concept of duty is inseparable from the belief that God exists and has a purpose in which we are involved;

(9) that an essential element in our attitude to the

created universe must be one of wonderment, awe and humility when we contemplate the infinite wisdom and inventiveness of God in creating, *ex nihilo*, the concepts of space and time, matter and mind, and above all of the mystery of life, and in devising such intricate laws to govern the interactions of these creations;

(10) that he has given us the power to know him partially by discovering these laws and applying them to create our individual characters and to mould our evolution in accordance with his will;

(11) that the purpose of all this creative activity has been to produce a race of beings made in God's image, ourselves, charged with the duty of defeating Satan, who with many other angels had rebelled against God and had been expelled from heaven, and of bringing them to repentance;

(12) that in waging war against Satan every victory is also a step towards building the kingdom of God on earth, and every reverse delays and impedes the achievement of this end;

(13) that although we have had a measure of success in carrying out this duty, we have also had many failures, and these have been particularly marked during the present century. More specifically, we have adopted false beliefs and have wrongfully used our power over our evolution to develop characteristics and to create conditions in which it is almost impossible for individuals to avoid sin, and which impede the performance of our duty and even in some measure reverse what had previously been achieved;

(14) that God, seeing that the task for which he had created the human race was proving to be beyond our powers, sent his Son to earth to guide us by his

teaching, to ease our task by depriving Satan temporarily of his eternal life (leaving him with temporal life), to assure us, by his crucifixion, that our link with God (the bond of obligation) will be maintained intact and receptive to his guidance provided that we repent of our wrongdoings, and by his resurrection to reassure us of our ultimate victory in the war against Satan;

(15) that when victory has been achieved and Satan and his followers have repented, we shall be rewarded by the gift of eternal life and admission to heaven, where we shall be given a new task, that of redeeming the fallen angels;

(16) and finally, that the accomplishment of our tasks on earth and in heaven will be accomplished by joy far beyond our present powers of understanding, joy which will increase as we learn, through the intermediacy of Christ, the infinite goodness and love of God the Father.

INDEX

Aaron 94
Abel 111
Abortion 6, 124
Abraham 8
Accidents,
   associated with substance 36, 90, 105
   at power stations 130
   in genetic research 131, 140
Action, freedom of 88
Adam 111, 112
Adolescence 67, 112
Adolescents 67, 99, 113, 142
Adoption 105
Africa, Southern 99, 100
Agag 5
Agape 22, 24, 70, 104, 137
Agnostics 101
Agriculture, use of chemicals in 99
Ahriman 84
Ahura Mazda 84
Aids virus 74
aionios 151
Alpha 56
Alphabet, four letter 29
Amalekites 5
Anaesthetics 36
Analogy 109–113
Angel of light 16
Angels,
   are co-eternal with God 23, 28, 114, 153
   are linked to God 53
   are sinful 23, 24
   as messengers 97, 154, 155
   'bad' 155, 156
   creation of 23, 114, 121
   disaffected 23, 25, 26, 65
   dwell in eternity 114
   evolution of 125
   existence of 24, 56, 133
   friendship with 157
   'good' 154–156
   guardian *see* guardian angels
   have eternal being 24
   have eternal life 28, 29, 103
   loyal 23, 26, 53
   malevolent 134
   minds of 153, 154
   rebellion of 23, 121, 158
   rebellious 16, 103
   redemption of 65, 103, 155–157, 160
Animals,
   appreciation of beauty by 42
   death of 25, 52
   domestic 44, 52
   domestication of 111
   experiments on 6
   have minds 15, 41
   instincts of 40, 42
   interdependence with plants 14
   killing of 30, 54
   mental activities of 41–43
   selective breeding and genetic engineering 44, 45
Anthropomorphism 122
aphesis 98
Apostles 95, 156
Apostles' Creed 103
Apostles, misleading 65
Approach, asymptotic 65, 107

Aquinas, St Thomas 115
Architecture 77, 157
Armoury 66–73
Army, God's 26, 27, 36, 43, 53, 55, 59, 60, 62, 67, 102
  final battle of 147
  in other worlds 64, 146, 147
Art,
  appreciation of 33, 36, 58, 76
  as agent of communication 66
  as experience of joy 157
  concept of 112
  destruction of works of 83
  in imagination 37, 157
  perversion of 76–79
  true purpose of 76–79, 157
Artefacts, imperfection of 100, 130
Articles, Thirty Nine 82
Artists, and predestination 61
Atheist 78, 101
Atmosphere, pollution of 99, 135, 139
Atom 49, 86, 100
Atonement 101
Augustine of Hippo, St 19
Authority,
  disregard for 119
  earthly 95–96
  higher 123
  international 131, 132
  rejection of 155
  tyrannical 126
Awareness 41, 45, 48–50, 53
Awe 27, 64, 146, 158, 159

Baby, birth of 54
Bacilli, destruction of 31
Beatitudes 5, 6, 79
Beauty,
  appreciation of 36, 37, 42
  concept of 37
Behaviour 12, 13, 32, 58, 59
Being,
  eternal *see* eternal being
  infinite 40

  of higher order 110
  physical 59
  spiritual 23
  temporal *see* temporal being
Beings, temporal 92
Belief(s),
  annihilation of 136
  creation of 73, 136
  current Christian 1–3, 90
  dictated by Satan 104
  false 16, 69, 70, 81–88, 98, 99, 159
  persistence of 82
  perversion of 79
Bethany 7, 8
Big bang 28
Birth, second 10, 11
Black holes 47
Body,
  accidents of 90, 105
  and mind, interaction of 34–39, 75
  as armour 66
  attacked by Satan 74, 75, 78
  frailty of 13, 68, 74
  has temporal being 13
  injury to 13, 66, 75
  is not evil 69, 84
  mortality of 13, 68
  spiritual 105
  substance of 90, 105, 141
  the temple of the Holy Spirit 74
  transformation of, for eternal life 141, 148–149, 153
Bond (channel) of obligation,
  admits Christ (Holy Spirit) to the soul 54, 86, 89, 125
  and concept of duty 53, 70
  and knowledge of God 53
  as passage for conscience 80
  blockage (obstruction) of 54, 70, 74, 89
  cleansing of 70, 86, 101, 125, 134, 139, 145, 147
  conveys God's instructions 53, 79

is unbreakable 53, 101
links angels to God 53, 54
opening of 102, 125, 139
our link with God 53, 101, 102, 125, 134, 139, 145, 147
Brains 38, 46
Brainwashing 89
Breeding, selective 44, 45
Buddhism 61, 132
Buddhist 101
Bully 25, 79, 122
Burning 82

Cain 111
Calamities 104, 106, 113, 125, 130, 140
Calvinists 17
Cancer 140
Capitalism 126, 128, 129
Carnivores 111–112, 135
Catastrophe 99, 143
Celibacy 18
Certainty 107, 145
Change,
  inevitability of 28
  recognition of need for 133–136
Channel of obligation *see* Bond (channel) of obligation
Character,
  change of 133
  creation of 136, 159
  defects of 117, 118
  development of 141
  expression of 22
  moulding of 27, 70, 73, 133
Charity 22, 79, 104
Chemicals 99
Child,
  death of 60
  mind of 73
  mind of, attacked by Satan 110
Childhood, abuses inflicted in 46
Child mortality 142
Children,
  assaults on 75

teaching of 59
their sense of fairness 58
upbringing of 71
Chimpanzee 42
Christ,
(for references to his life on earth *see* Jesus Christ)
  admission of 89, 103, 119, 122, 125, 133
  belief in 11
  dwelling in us 60, 86
  friendship with 157
  guidance of 72, 89, 137, 145
  has two natures, two wills 3
  his instructions 53
  his leadership 147
  his readiness to respond 55
  his unity with the Father 8, 92
  his will 105
  one with 105
  our advocate 97, 149
  our Commander 107
  our friend 3
  our leader 108
  presence of 62
  second coming of 18
  stands at the door 70
  supreme on earth 108
  the captain of our souls 147
  the Commander-in-Chief 55
  unity with 109
Christian communities 95
Christian community, spread of 138
Christianity,
  asserts God's purpose 1
  basic truths of 133
  distinguishing features of 1
  foundation of 1
  rise of 82
  teaching of 84
Christians 90, 102
Church and state, conflict of 61
Church,
  Anglican 82

163

early 82
enrichment of 84
  Roman Catholic 143
  teaching of 82
Church councils 3
Civilians, killing of 5
Civilisation, advance of 61
Climate, change in 99, 135
Clothing, provision of 85
Code, normative 81
Coleridge, Samuel 31
Comforter 11
Commandment 96
Commandment,
  breach of 117
Commandments,
  extended by Christ 2
  the ten: 2, 117, 124
  the ten, inadequacy of 4
Communal action 4
Communal sin 119
Communal will 19
Communication, spiritual 65, 137, 141, 143, 147, 152
Communication, telepathic 137
Communism 84, 126, 128, 129
Community 62, 98
Community, punishment of 119
Competition 14, 79, 108, 125, 150
Complexity 25, 49–50
Complexity, urge towards 49
Comprehension 38
Computer 86, 131, 135
Computer technology 47
Comradeship 102
Conscience 9, 39–40, 80, 87
Conscience,
  as parent of desire 80
  a spiritual faculty 39, 80
  damaged by Satan 75
  fallibility of 9, 39
  meaning of 80
  of angels 23
  perversion of 79
  the gifts of the Holy Spirit 39

Consciousness 25, 33, 41, 45, 48–9
Consciousness,
  in complexity 50
  in atomic 48
  substance of 50–1
  surface of 38
  total 50
  units of 50–1
Consequences,
  adverse 100
  disastrous 130
  harmful 67, 82, 98
  temporal 98
Constraint, freedom from 53, 72
Context, secular 78
Contingent code 124–5
Contraception 143
Convent 133
Conventions, social 113
Co-operation 14, 109
Counsellor 3
Countries,
  advanced 139–40
  less developed 140
Courage 27
Created beings,
  have value 44
  their role in God's plan 44
Created in God's image 148, 159
Created world, good but imperfect 115
Creation of man 149
Creation, the 113, 114, 121
Creatures,
  development of 125
  have value 44
  involved in God's purpose 44
  living 51
  mental faculties of 45
  none is vile 44
  preservation of 30
Creed, adherence to 101
Creed, Apostles' 103
Creed, sectarian 83
Cross, the 2, 19, 96
Cross, the, meaning of 102

Crucifixion, the 1, 2, 8, 83, 96, 144, 147, 160,
Cruelty 80, 83, 122
Culture 61, 66, 73, 128
Culture,
　avant-garde 76
　common 72, 73–4
　Western 7

Damage,
　ecological 131, 142
　psychological 128
　spiritual 128
Damnation 63
Danger, freedom from 73
Darwin, Charles 36
David 118
Death,
　abolished 102
　conquest of 102–3
　earthly 68, 102
　moment of 90
　mystery of 102
　of living creatures 25, 52
　way of 100
Debauchery 59
Debt, meaning of 120
Decisions,
　communal 66
　made by the soul 66
　mental 66
　spiritual 66
Dedication, Feast of 8
Deeds, wrongful 117
Deity, lesser 84
De Libero Arbitrio (St Augustine) 19
Delight 33
Denominations, Christian 132
Dependents, care for 15
Depression 13, 36
Desire,
　counter 22
　sexual 21
　to conform to a norm 81
　to dominate 79

Desires,
　annihilation of 73, 136
　complex of 81
　conforming with duty 27
　creation of 73, 136
　evil 69, 70
　modification of 136
　natural 73, 75
　perversion of 79
　relation to beliefs 81
　unnatural 75
Destiny,
　of human race 30, 88, 109
　ultimate 38, 97
Determination, spiritual 40
Determinism 47
Devices,
　electronic 127, 140
　mechanical 127
Dictatorship 79
Dimension,
　new 89
　spiritual 40
Disability, physical 74
Disaster,
　as consequence of false vision 106
　as consequence of usurping God's powers 141
　avoidance of 108
　in history 62
　prevented by God's intervention 100
Disciples, power of 95
Discipline,
　in child rearing 71
　of the church 138
Discomfort 121
Disease,
　cure for 86
　liability to 68
　prevention of 30
　viral 100
Diseases, respiratory 99
Disorders,

physical 142
psychological 117, 139, 141–2
pulmonary 140
Displeasure 233
Dissensions 59
Distress 33
Distrust 33
Divine principles 126
Divorce 75, 124
DNA 29
Doctrine 3, 82, 83, 88
Doctrine, importance of 126
Dogs,
  homing instinct of 42
  rescue by 40
Domestication of animals 44
Domination 63, 79, 122, 150
Double helix 29
Down's syndrome 74
Drink 73
Drinking bouts 59
Drought 73
Drug abuse 119
Drug culture 99
Drugs 36, 75, 78
Dualism 18
Duties 57, 62, 88, 89, 158
Duties,
  communal 31
  individuals 31
  twofold 125
Duty 21, 26, 27, 28, 30, 39, 40, 41, 53, 54, 55, 60, 70, 81, 121, 134, 146, 148, 151
Duty,
  concept of 39, 70, 110, 116, 134, 158, 159
  definition of 134
  discharge of 120
  military aspect of 63
  performance of 159
  to love God 70
  to our neighbour 70

Ears, damage to 78

Earth,
  insignificance of 30
  preservation of 143
  structure of 100
Earthly death 52, 150
Earthly life 141, 149
Earthquakes 14, 115
Eastern bloc 128
Ecology 132
Economic factors 139
Economics 125–29
Economics, dominance of 60, 99, 109, 125
Economics, western 7
Economic system, new 126–7, 129
Economic system, rules of 126, 127
Economic systems 104
Ecstasy 33
Eden, Garden of 15, 111
Efficiency 127
Effort, common 60
Election 17f, 19
Electronic devices 48
Elements, radioactive 100
Elijah 94, 95, 138
Elisha 94, 138
Elizabeth I, Queen 83, 88
Emotion 33
Emotions 136
Emotions, experience of 41
Empires 61
Employment, provision of 85
End of Time, The (Pieper) 62
Endor, witch of 5
Enemies, commandment to love 5
Enemy 59, 64, 71
Energy 100, 114, 130
Energy,
  creation of 28
  solar 130
  sources of 130
  tidal 130
  world of 33
Enoch 94
Entities, natural and spiritual 51

Environment 60, 73, 74, 123, 133
Environment, damage to 15, 139
Environmental factors 59
Envy 24, 33, 59, 155
Epidemic 89, 140
Equality 62, 63
Equipment,
  faulty 12, 14
  necessarily imperfect 12
Eros 137
Errors, political and social 67
Eternal being 3, 24, 25, 28, 49, 51, 52, 65, 67, 90, 103, 114, 133, 141, 146, 149, 156
Eternal being, defined 13
Eternal beings,
  are free 23, 72
  their relation to sin 116
Eternal life 2, 10–11, 28, 62, 89, 90, 98, 101, 103, 108, 114, 136, 138, 147, 148,149, 150, 151, 156
Eternal life,
  adaptation to 153
  available to all 102
  bodily difficulties in 153
  concept of 105, 151
  definition of 90
  gift of 11, 160
  held in reserve 104
  is a seed 104
  is infinite 104
  is more abundant 105
  mental difficulties in 153
  responsibilities of 89
  seed of 147
Eternal order 78, 136
Eternal realm 72
Eternity 38, 40, 90, 109, 114, 136, 137, 147, 150, 151, 155
Eternity,
  a medium for being 28
  and time, analogy for 151
  and time, link between 150
  damaged by Satan 121
  event in 101

further work in 65
infection of 121
is unbounded 56
journey through 152
proceeds from God 28, 114, 151
Ethic,
  distorted 63
  false 69
Euthanasia 124
Evil 15, 16
Evil,
  existence of 69
  meaning of 114, 115–6
  mystery of 113
  problem of 108
  propensity to 69
  relation to sin 115
  responsibility for 83, 114
  root of 85
  Spirit of 84
Evils,
  ecological 104
  social 104
Evolution 58, 114, 125, 133, 149
Evolution,
  biological 135
  course of 141
  direction of 27, 67, 70, 103
  human 134, 149
  laws of 31, 32, 41, 51, 52, 73, 149
  moulding of 73, 136, 159
  progress in 154
Evolutionary chain 51
Exaltation 33
Example to children 71
Excitement 33
Expiation 101
Extra-terrestrial beings 65, 146, 147
Eyes, damage to 78

Facilities, medical 139
Factors, genetic and environmental 64
Faculties 60, 64, 67, 73, 75, 81, 98
Faculties,

annulment of 73
bodily 149
creation of 73
mental 149, 153
of other species 42
restrained by God 42
submerged by intellect 42
Fairness, sense of 58
Faith 72, 79, 104
Faith, necessity of 68
Faiths, other 90
Fall, the 43
Familiarity breeds neglect 41
Father, the 92, 97, 101, 105
Fear 33, 37, 80
Fertilisation, moment of 54
Fertility, control of 142–3
Fidelity 59
Films 131
Final Cause 31
Fire, everlasting 10
Fires 115
Fish 114
Fission, propagation by 49
Flesh 69
Flesh and blood 59
Flesh, at war with the Spirit 18
Flood, the 112
Floods 115
Foetus 61
Foetus, not sinful 115
Folly 131, 135
fons et origo 116
Food 30
Food,
  desire for 73
  provision of 85
Force, directional 31
Foreknowledge 18, 61
Forgiveness 97, 98, 100
Fornication 59
Frailty 78
Freedom 51, 121, 144, 148
Freedom,
  curtailment of 132

encroachment on 125
enhanced 136
greater 150, 151, 53
of angels 23
of the soul 39
Free will 12, 17, 19, 123
Friendship 157
Fruit, forbidden 111
Fuel rods 131
Future generations, punishment
  falling on 31

Gabriel 23
Galations 59
Galaxy 100
Galilee 92
Gangsta-rap 78
Genealogies 69
Generations, future 31
Generations, future *see also*
  Posterity
Genes 6, 39
Genesis 27, 109, 111, 112, 149
Genetic engineering 6, 44, 135
Genetic experiments 131
Genetic factors 59
Genetic features 117
Genetic research 135, 140
Genetic structure 133
Gentleness 59
Gluttony 75
Gnostics 69
Goal,
  of eternal life 89
  of humanity 62, 71
Goals, materialistic 128
God,
  access to 70
  admission of 15
  alienation from 2, 76
  a living Being 1
  alliance with 51
  alone is perfect 23
  a loving Father 61
  answerability to 46

a rational Being 59
being of, supra-eternal 114
broke his commandment 5
children of 105, 149
commandment to love 2
constraint by 12, 22, 100, 102
duty to 89
duty to love 70
dwells in supra-eternity 56f
enemies of 83
evidence of 1
existence of *see* 'his existence', below
failure to consult 87
foresight of 68
frustration of his plan 15, 24
frustration of his will 13
gave his Son 17
grace of 27, 100, 102
has authority 158
has a will 1, 21
his accomplishment 96
his apostles 156
his armies 147
his army 26, 27, 36, 43, 53, 55, 59, 60, 62, 64, 102
his army, other beings in 64, 147
his benevolence 139
his bounty 37, 110
his commandments, breach of 66
his commands 55
his creation 74, 126
his creative activity 52
his creative power 32
his divine nature 31
his essence,
　expressed as love 92
　expressed by the gift of eternal life 104
　falling short of, as the meaning of evil 114
　implies the existence of angels 56
　is love 158
　its link with suffering 121
　love as an approximation to 21

our power to reflect 54
rendered inactive 104
revealed by science 85
revealed by the world 14
revealed in art 55, 76, 78, 112, 157
revealed in a secular context 78
understanding of 55
his existence,
　assumption of 1
　awareness of 53
　evidence of 37
　experience of 49
　is supra-eternal 133
　rational grounds for 49
his foreknowledge 18, 19, 61
his further purpose 151
his glory 58, 146
his goodness 19, 20, 160
his grace 27, 100, 102
his grand design 129
his guidance 63, 71, 73, 91, 148
his handiwork in nature 36
his handiwork, marred 44
his help 63, 71
his incarnation 1, 91–96, 103, 144
his instructions 54, 64, 70, 152
his interventions 91–105
his inventiveness 41
his invisible powers 31
his kingdom *see* Kingdom of God
his laws,
　operation of 119
　tampering with 119
　use of, by Satan 144
his love,
　angels, as recipients of 23, 121
　conveyed to our souls 54
　must have an object 23, 158
　negative response to 155
　positive response to 154
　reflexion of 23
　rejection of 23
　response to 22, 23, 64, 154, 158
　testimony to 102

the essence of his Personality
　　　　21, 22
his majesty 146
his nature 15
his omnipotence 19, 114, 121
his omniscience 18, 19
his overall plan 26, 45, 52
his plan 23, 25, 30, 34, 37, 44, 61,
　　65, 79, 95, 122, 125, 149, 154
his plan, frustration of 15, 24
his power over death 95
his power over earthly authorities
　　95
his power to forgive 96
his power, surrender of 54
his providence 107
his purpose,
　　achievement of 43
　　and predestination 19, 61
　　contribution to, by different
　　　　species 43
　　defeat of 145
　　frustration of 19, 95, 148
　　fulfilment of 19, 92, 133, 134,
　　　　146, 152, 156
　　governs his actions 21, 146
　　implied by his will 1, 21
　　in creating humanity 59, 102, 158
　　in creating individuals 19
　　individual tasks in fulfilling 61
　　knowledge of 150
　　our armoury adequate for 66–7
　　our duty to discover 148
　　our failure to understand 19
　　our role in 102, 134, 148
　　riddle of 148
　　to restore harmony in heaven
　　　　155, 158
　　understanding of 138
his response to prayer 91, 144, 148
his secrets 45, 148
his soldiers 64, 67, 156
his strategy 26, 27, 28–9, 33, 43,
　　53, 55
his strategy,

　　final stage of 51, 53
　　opposition to 54
　　was predictable 56
his subsidiary plan 25, 26, 45
his suffering 121, 122
his sustaining activity 13, 31, 51,
　　52, 54, 90, 103
his ultimate objective 56
his ultimate purpose 155
his will see Will of God
his wisdom 159
his wrath 122
imposes restraints 42, 72, 136, 137
insult to 127
interference by 12
interventions by 91–105, 130, 144
is compassionate 17
is good 63
is infinite 55
is just 18
is love 18, 21, 56, 70, 92, 121, 158
is patient 44
is perfect 23
is three Persons 1, 133
kingdom of see Kingdom of God
knowledge of 152, 158
Lamb of 97
laws of 28, 34
obedience to 69
obligation to 30
our power to compel 54
our relation to 89, 105, 144, 148
our service to 108, 148, 156
praise of 36–7
rejection of 3, 128
response by 22, 23, 158
response to his love 22, 23, 158
responsibility of 114
revelation of 14, 15
revelation of his kingdom 106
soldiers in his army 36, 43, 46,
　　53, 55, 60, 68, 92, 98, 144
submission to 69
sustaining activity of 13, 31, 51,
　　52, 54, 90, 103

the abode of truth 88
the Creator 3, 158
the Father 149, 158, 160
understanding of 138
unfavourable depiction of 11, 17
voice of 107
war with 26
will not destroy himself 104
will not destroy his creation 25, 31, 52
world not opposed to 15
God, lesser, the author of evil 69
Gods,
  appeasement of 112
  existence of 112
  false 2
Good and evil 34, 40, 110, 136
Goodness 20, 59
Goodness, concept of 37, 116
Good, Spirit of 84
Gospel, preaching of 95
Government, forms of 61
Grace, adoption and 105
Grace, fall from 15
Greed 31, 131
Greeks 103
Grief 60
Group 60, 73, 74, 81, 83
Group, philosophy of 78
Guardian angels 155
Guidance, duty to provide 76

Half-life 100
hamartias 117, 120
Happiness 33, 157
Happiness, pursuit of 109
Hardship 27
Harmony,
  in heaven 91, 103, 155, 158
  universal 129
Hatred 33
Healing, miraculous 93, 138–141
Healing the sick 7, 96
Health 35, 135
Health care 140

Health services 139
Heat, reaction to 33
Heaven 148, 150, 152
Heaven,
  admission to 3, 160
  corruption of 24
  disharmony in 158
  harmony in 91, 103, 155, 158
  journey towards 90
  life in 148, 157
  no marriage in 149
  rejoicing in 65
  tasks in 148
  war in 23, 155
Hegel, Georg W.F. 84
Hell 103, 147
Herbivore 135
Heredity 123
Heresy, dualist 18
Heretics 9
Herod 93
Heroism 81
Hindu 101
Historian 132
History 61
Holocaust 83
Holy Ghost 97
Holy Spirit 3, 39, 54, 70, 82, 101
Holy Spirit,
  cleansing power of 70, 86, 101, 103, 133, 134, 139, 145
  gift of 143
  gift of healing by 138
  guidance of 143
  power of 138, 143
  sin against 102
Homing instinct 42
Honey 14
Hope 35, 79, 104
Hope, renewal of 106
Hosea 87
Hubris 135
Human being, death of 25, 52
Human beings,
  affinity with animals 19

alone have conscience 39
attacked by Satan 110
awareness in 49
created in God's image 6, 54
creation of 28, 51, 52
equated with machines 127
frailty of 78
have souls 6
interference by 44
not perfectible 107
their distinction from other
    animals 110
their role in God's plan 26, 158
Humanity,
  goal of 62
  survival of 87
Humankind,
  benefits to 82
  creation of 51, 142
  destiny of 88
  its assigned destiny 109
  its true function 128
  origin of 109
  sinfulness of 43, 97, 122
  ultimate destiny of 129
Human nature,
  divine principles in 126
  is not evil 69
Human race,
  affected by the Incarnation 1
  ancestors of 149
  annihilation of 130
  creation of 28, 51, 142, 154
  death of 134
  destruction of 103
  evolution of 67, 133
  honoured by God 27
  immaturity of 136
  insignificance of 27
  involved in God's purpose 1
  reason for its creation 38
  rebelliousness of 112
  tasks of 21
Human species, preservation of 153
Humility 33, 46, 139, 146, 159

Hurricane 115
Hymns 36–7
Hyperactivity 36
Hypocrisy 87

Icons 112
Ideas, abstract 37
Identity, awareness of 41
Idolatry 59
Idols 87
Illogicality 87
Images, destruction of 83
Imagination 33, 37
Immaturity, state of 91, 96
Immediate ends 52
Immortality 102
Imperfection 64
Incarnation, the 1, 91, 92, 144
Income, equality of 85
Indecency 59
Individuality 63
Individual,
  preservation 47, 122, 154
  survival of 36
Indulgences 84
Infant 60
Infant, innocence of 110
Infinity 104
Information 29
Information technology 9
Ingenuity, human 128
Initiative 144, 148
Initiative, rests with us 70, 144, 148
Inquiry, scientific 85
Inquisition, the 9, 83–4
Instinct 14, 40, 42, 110
Instinct,
  homing 42
  of self-preservation 58
  sexual 58
Institutions, human 125
Intellect, conflict with soul 78
Intellect, pre-eminence of 110
Intellectual experiences 42
Interaction 66

Interactive laws 28, 34, 47, 51
Intercourse, sexual 142, 143
Interdependence 14, 108, 125, 127, 150
Interests, trivial 99
Interest, vested 107
Internal combustion engine 86, 99, 135
Internet, the 86, 131
Intrigues, party 59
Inventiveness,
  of God 41
  of human beings 33, 43
Ireland, Northern 83
Isaiah 93
Islam 132

Jain 101
Jairus 94
James I 88
Jealousy 24, 59, 155
Jeremiah 93
Jericho 7, 8
Jerusalem 7, 8
Jerusalem, New 71
Jesus Christ,
  admits Satan's power 75
  amplified the commandments 2, 5
  arrest of 4
  baptism of 7
  empowered his disciples to remit sins 96
  encountered Satan 103
  expelled the moneylenders 8
  forgave sins 91
  had no dependents 8
  had no earthly father 93
  had no home 8
  healed the sick 7, 74, 93, 96, 142
  his ascension 1, 91, 94
  his crucifixion 1, 83, 96, 98, 144, 147, 160
  his death 2, 19, 91, 95–97, 134, 156
  his descent into hell 103, 144, 147
  his divinity, evidence 92–96
  his resurrection 1, 2, 91, 93–97, 105
  life of 7–9
  proclaimed as Christ 93
  temptation of 155
  the incarnation of God 1, 91, 92, 95, 96, 144
Jesus Christ *see* also Christ
Jet propulsion 86
Jews,
  belief in afterlife 90, 102
  can attain eternal life 101
  their special role 83
John the Baptist 93, 97
John the disciple 97
Joseph 97, 101
Joy 31, 33, 59, 109, 157, 160
Judaea 7
Judaism 132
Judgement,
  of ourselves 118
  perversion of 66, 76
  reserved to God 118, 120
  unaided 66
Justice, administration of 71
Juvenal 75

Killing, wanton 31
Kindness 59
Kingdom of God 106–9
Kingdom of God,
  admission to 10
  building of,
    a crusade 71
    a formidable task 67
    a slow process 133
    can never be complete 65
    encouraged by art 78
    God's help in 55
    impeded by wrong objectives 74
    is assured 104
    linked to enlightenment 96, 113

    linked to fertility control 142
    linked to lifting of restraints 73
    linked to soul cleansing 89
    promoted by spiritual
        communication 137
    resumption of 106
    start of 133
    will lessen communal sin 119
    will lessen desire to dominate
        122
    will lessen suffering 122
  conditions in, known only to
      God 63
  establishment of 4
  has many features 107
  inheritance of 59
  is distinct from utopia 63, 106
  is perfect 65
  knowledge of its nature 106
  not fully attainable 107
  partial building of 64
  prevalence of virtue in 104
  the new Jerusalem 71
Kingdom of heaven 9, 96
Knowledge,
  advances in 86
  deficiency of 46
  empirical 35
  false assumption of 46
  of God 152, 158
  of the past 151–2
  partial 153
  power of 33
  repository of 38
  tree of 111
  urge for 30

Labour, shortage of 129
Lamb of God 97
Land, set aside 99
Language,
  common 137
  misuse of 116
  sign 42
  structure of 38
  understanding of 34
Language of the world 24
Last Supper, the 97
Law 123
Law,
  conformity with 113
  higher 127
  international 132
  natural 142, 143, 144
Laws,
  divine 28
  evolutionary 51
  interaction of 28
  interactive 34, 47, 51
  physical 29, 47, 49
  psychical 51
Lawyer 132
Lazarus 8, 93
Leisure 60
Leprosy 94
Liberty 62, 63
Life,
  after death 57, 82, 89–90, 95
  antagonisms to 14
  brevity of 13
  continuation of 68
  creation of 29, 49, 52
  earthly 50, 58, 89, 90
  eternal *see* Eternal life
  evolution of 49
  expectation of 142
  in heaven 148
  in the universe 29, 64, 146–7
  is information 29
  meaning of 62
  modern, strain of 9
  mystery of 102, 159
  next stage of 50
  on earth, study of 30
  origin of 29
  outlook on 28
  pattern of 6, 74
  preservation of 47
  quality of 11
  temporal 29, 51, 89, 90, 108, 114

variety of 42
way of 100
Lifestyle, simplified 9
Limbs, defective 138
Limbs, malformation of 74
Literature 157
Living creatures, subject to law 51
Living matter, building blocks of 49
Living, pattern of 30
Living species, preservation of 30
Living, standard of 85, 86
Logic 38
Lord's prayer, the 117, 120
Lot 8
Love 33, 59
Love,
  agapeic 40, 45, 70, 156
  an act of will 22
  as an emotion 21
  being in 137
  divine 147
  is not reflexive 22–3
  is outgoing 22
  meaning of 21–2
  parental 60
  trivial meaning of 21
  unrequited 121
Luke, St 95
Lust 33, 75

Male and female, distinguished in heaven 149
Malefactor, penitent 93
Malice 155
Mammon 65, 77
Mammon, worship of 109
Man, insignificance of 27
Marital breakdown 79, 119
Martha 8, 93
Marx, Karl 84, 126
Mary (mother of Jesus) 8, 97, 139, 153
Mary, Queen 83
Mary (sister of Lazarus) 8
Materialism, scientific 128

Mathematical truth 37
Mathematics 34
Mathematics, pure 79
Matter 114
Matter and energy, being of 27
Matter and mind,
  concepts of 159
  interaction of 46
Matter and mind *see also* Body and mind
Matter,
  creation of 28
  has temporal being 34
  substance of 34, 46, 51
Maturity, growth in 73, 113, 115, 136
Measures, draconian 132
Mechanical device 78
Medicine, orthodox 140
Medium, multidimensional 151
Medium, spiritual 66
Meekness 5
Meek, the, are blessed 79
Members of one body 60
Memories, fictitious 46
Memory 33, 38, 52
Memory, is fallible 152
Mental activities 41, 50
Mental communication 65
Mental difficulties 153
Mental disorders 9, 46, 117
Mental disorders *see also* Psychological disorders
Mental experiences 33, 34–5, 50
Mental experiences,
  extra-sensory 36
  inseparable from consciousness 50
Mental faculties,
  are units of consciousness 50
  of other species 41, 45
  restrained by God 42, 46
  submerged by intellect 42
  use of 41
Mental powers, latent 42

Mental powers, range of 47
Mental substance 46, 89, 90, 105, 141, 149, 156
Mentors 156
Mercy 11
Messages, spiritual 154, 156
Messiah 8
metanoia 91, 99
metanoiein 130
Meteors 29
Michael 23, 26, 155
Mind,
  activities of 154
  and soul, interaction of 38
  as armoury 66
  as intermediary 38
  attacked by Satan 74
  communal 82
  complexity of 64
  conscious 46
  content of 73
  creation of 33-4, 52, 156
  damage to 76
  date of creation unknown 33, 45
  further dimension of 154
  gateway to the soul 75
  has temporal being 34
  has implantation of 154
  intangible nature of 46
  its conflict with the soul 38
  laws of 45, 47
  linked with matter 33, 34
  mortality of 68
  of animals 41
  operation of 80
  spiritual 68, 105
  subconscious 46
  subject to disease 13
  substance of 34, 45
  task of 12
  the repository of knowledge 38
  two levels of 46
  weakness of 68
Minorities, protection of 124
Miracles 72, 74, 91, 93, 136, 143

Miracles, healing 138-41, 143-4
Miraculous gifts 143-4
Misery 33
Mistakes, freedom from making 144
Mistakes, learning from 67, 98, 106, 124, 130, 144
Modern life, complexities of 124
Modern life, stresses of 9
Molecules, urge to form 49
Moloch 77
Monastery 133
Money, love of 74, 85
Moral absolutes 9
Moral code 122-3, 124-5
Moral confusion 118
Moral imperative 6
Moral issues 7, 39, 58
Moral problems 124
Moral sense 33, 40, 48, 58, 154
Moral theory 55
Morrow, thought for the 9
Mortality 78, 142
Moses 95
Murder 75
Music 33, 58, 112, 157
Music,
  debasement of 77-8
  sacred 78
Muslims 90, 101
Mutations 73, 139
Mystery 96, 98, 102, 103
Mysticism 157

Nain, widow of 93
Nation 61
Natural law 92, 143, 144
Natural selection 14, 36, 44-5, 58
Nature,
  beauty of 36-7
  enjoyment of 36
  wonders of 36
Nazareth 8, 140
Nazis 83
Necessity of imperfection 12

Neighbour, commandment to love
   2, 4, 5, 22
Neighbours,
   duty to love 70, 82, 96
   personal relations with 77
Nervous system 38, 46
New Testament 10–11, 97, 101
Newton, Isaac 15
Nicodemus 97
Non-agricultural use of land 99
Non-living beings, mind in 47
Non-living world,
   evolution of 45
   mental activity in 45
Nuclear power 100
Nuclear power stations 140
Nuclear war 130
Number, understanding of 42

Objective,
   at the end of time 32
   common 56, 60, 82
   consequences of 67
   evolution directed to 31
   false 67
   true 109, 157
   ultimate 90
Objectives,
   cleansed in Purgatory 149
   dictated by Satan 104
   false 16, 118–20, 123
   formulation of 12
   furtherance of 39
   long term 74
   power to choose 136
   selection of 73
   wrong 98
Obligation,
   bond of *see* Bond of obligation
   channel of *see* Channel of obligation
   concept of 53
   to God 30, 49
Obsessions 13
Obstacles 70

Offender, reform of 120
Offensive 147
Old people, proportion of 139
Old Testament 11, 87
Omega 56f
Onslaught, final 147
opheilma 120
Opinions, of others 88
Opponent, mind of 66
Organism,
   complex 50
   pathogenic 74
Orgies 59
Origen 138, 144
Original sin 123
Ormuzd 84
Orphans 2
'ought',
   concept of 134
   deletion of 134, 135
   restoration of 135
Outlook, secular 65

Pain 13, 33, 35, 58, 121
Pain, ability to feel 12
Parables 96
Paraclete 3, 11
Paranoia 13
Parents 60
Particle 31, 49
Past events 152
Past, knowledge of 151–2
Pathogenic organisms 139
Paths, false 71
Patience 59
Paul, St,
   advises young people 69
   predestination 17–18
   and the dualist heresy 18
   describes our enemies 59
   his advice to Timothy 27
   his commitment to the gospel 18
   ignores genetic factors 59
   is not infallible 18
   on our being members of one

body 60
on our knowledge of God 153
on the body as the temple of the Holy Spirit 74
on the gifts of the Spirit 58
on the love of money 85
on the power of the Holy Spirit 144
on the redemptive power of the Cross 97
on the revelation of God 31
opposed 'the flesh' to 'the spirit' 69
performed miracles 138
warned Timothy 69
Peace,
lover of 62
the harvest of the Spirit 59
Penalties 120
People, group of 60, 73–4, 81, 83
Perception 32–4
Perception, sensory 35, 36
Perfection,
is unreachable 65, 89
progress towards 89
Persuasion 74
Pessimists 107
Peter, St 69, 93, 138
Petitions, individual 56
Phenomenon of Man, The (Teilhard de Chardin) 48
Philip, St 138
Philosophers 61, 132, 143, 157
Philosophic systems 37
Philosophy 34, 55
Phobias 13
Physical being 59
Physical entity 51
Physical law 32, 47, 49, 51
Physical particles 48, 50
Physical particles, consciousness in 48
Physical world 34
Pieper, Josef 62
Pilgrimage 12

Plagues 122, 140
Planet 100
Plant, death of 25, 52
Plants 114, 137
Plants,
killing of 30, 54
mind dwelling in 47
receive telepathic messages 47
Pleasure 33, 37, 58, 157
Pleasure, capacity to experience 121
Poetry 112
Political systems 7
Politicians 143
Politics 55
Pollution 99
Pope, the 82
Population,
increase of 139
world 100, 142, 143
Posterity 99, 100, 113
Posterity, Ministry for 131–3
Power,
love of 74
nuclear 100
Powers,
as our enemy 59
latent 136, 138
thaumaturgic 145
usurpation of 141
Power stations 130, 131
Pragmatism 126
Praise 89
prayer,
consulting God in 87
false ending to 105, 134
for enlightenment 107
for God's help 71
for knowledge of God 158
for strength and courage 133–5
God's response to 91, 144, 148
meaning of 71
power of 134
Predestination 17–20, 61
Press-gang 62
Pride 33

Primitive people 139
Principalities 59
Problems,
   metaphysical 128
   moral 6, 101
   personal 59
Profession 61
Progress, technological 86
Propagation 38, 49
Prophecies, false 16
Prophetical books 87
Propitiation 97, 101
Protestants, burning of 83
Psalmist 27
Psychoanalysts 46
Psychical entity 51
Psychical law 47, 51
Psychical particles 50
Psychological disorders 37, 139–42
Psychological disorders *see also* Mental disorders
Psychology 132
Psycho-physical interaction 36
Psycho-physical interaction *see also* Body and mind, Matter and Mind
Public, gullibility of 76
Punishment 31, 62, 119, 120, 122
Punishment eternal 10, 11, 17, 19
Purgatory 3, 4, 84, 149
Purpose,
   concept of 38
   God's, individual tasks in 61
   in the creation of life 29
   in relation to the test theory 59, 62
   of our creation 63, 71
Purpose *see also* God, his purpose

Quarrelling,
   between sects 83
   in heaven 155
Question, fundamental 157
Quick and the dead, the 2

Race, one held responsible for all evil 83
Radiation 100
Radio 86
Rage, fits of 59
Ransom 97
Raphael 23
Rave 77
Reaction to distant events 32
Reality,
   expansion of 33
   foreordained 56
Reason, power of 49
Rebellion, state of 147
Redemption 104, 155
Reflex action 47
Relationships, personal 131
Religions,
   Eastern 102
   multiplicity of 83
   non-theistic 61
   quarrelling in 83
Religious subjects, portrayal of 78
Remission,
   of sin 98, 100, 102
   of time 84
Repentance 91, 98, 102, 130, 147, 155
Research, scientific 85, 141
Resentment 33
Response, compelled 23, 148
Responsibilities, new 150
Responsibility,
   assumption of 15
   extent of 59
Restraint,
   complete freedom from 141
   faculties held in 42, 143
   on our thaumaturgic power 91
   our souls subject to 72, 158
Restraints 136–42
Restraints, lifting of 133, 158
Resurrection 1, 2, 91, 93, 95–6, 105, 138
Retribution 80

Revelation,
  divine 88
  further 11
  gradual 124
Revenge 80, 98, 120
Rewards 120
Riches, danger of 11
Ridley, Matt 29
Right, absolute and contingent 142
Right and wrong,
  categories of 40
  coincidence with good and evil 40
  concept of 40, 80
  consequences of doing 58
  content of 80
  confusion of 110, 124
  displayed by other species 39
  distinction between 9, 40, 110, 136
  distinction between, blurred 17, 119
  idea of 58
  knowledge of 110
  link with conscience 39, 80
  natural origin of 39
  sense of 40, 58
  understanding of 33
Righteousness,
  agents of 16
  growth in 65
Role, fulfilment of 90
Roman Catholics 83
Roman Empire 95
Rule, divine 70

Sacrifice 27, 72
Sahara desert, the 130
Saints 80

Salvation,
  available to everyone 102
  communal 4
  conferred by doctrine 83
  impeded by wealth 11
  journey to 108
  of all 10
  of humankind 62, 71, 85, 97
  personal 3, 17, 71, 85
  ultimate 61
Samuel 5, 118
Sapphira 138
sarx 18, 69
Satan,
  abandons ground 63
  a fallen angel 72
  alienates us from God 77
  alliance with 51
  cannot prevail 103
  command of 134
  conquest of 135
  contest with 25
  damaged the environment 14
  damaged the souls of our ancestors 15
  defeat of 26, 33, 41, 53, 59, 61, 65, 67, 68, 83, 100, 103–7, 121, 122, 147, 151, 156, 159
  deprived of eternal life 103, 104, 144, 160
  destruction of 25
  disarmed 103, 104
  encountered by God 103
  encourages conflict 61
  existence of 68–9
  expulsion of 23–4
  final assault on 64, 147
  has access to our souls 68
  has damaged eternity 121
  has eternal being 67, 72, 103
  his advantages 67–8, 70, 72
  his agents 64, 77
  his attack,
    on our aesthetic sense 75–9
    on our beliefs 81–8
    on our bodies 74–5, 77, 89
    on our desires 79–81
    on our minds 74, 75–89
    on our souls 74
  his attacks repulsed 70
  his changing tactics 76, 124

his defeat certain 108, 111
his eternal life 103, 147
his handiwork 13
his influence in heaven 24
his influence on electronic devices
    48
his lieutenants 64, 146–7
his military strategies 26
his mode of being 68, 74, 103
his power 66, 146
his rage 123
his sense of humour 77
his tactics 74–91, 136
his thaumaturgic power 73, 74,
    89
his use of natural law 144
his weapons 66, 67–8, 88–9
his wiliness 84, 146
idea of, dismissed 63
is invisible 59, 69
is not encumbered 68
is not linked to God 105
is our enemy 71
masquerades as God (or as an
    angel of light) 5f, 16, 76, 81
misleads us 13
on a par with our souls 68, 103
ontological equality with 68
partially disarmed 134
persuades us that he does not
    exist 68, 81
perverts our judgement of art and
    music 76–7
privilege denied to 70
rebellion of 23, 24, 56, 155
redemption of 25, 26, 59, 64, 68,
    100, 122, 134, 147
repentance of 64, 68, 134, 159
resistance to 10
roams freely 15
surrender of 65
uncertain of victory 72
varies his attacks 76, 82
victory by 87, 103
victory over 37, 60, 71, 103

voice of 107
war against 23, 26, 31, 37, 53, 56,
    60, 62, 65, 67, 68, 90, 103,
    106, 130, 134, 136, 137, 144,
    148, 155, 159
war with, on our part defensive
    69
Saul 5, 118
Schizophrenia 13
Science 130–5
Science,
    advances in 113
    as a panacea 85–6, 130
    can reveal God's essence 85
Scientific methods 78
Scientists 6
Scientists, their power to create life
    29
Self-consciousness 41
Self-control 59
Self-defence 4
Self-importance 58
Self-interest 154
Self-policing system 129
Self-preservation 32
Self-sacrifice 81
Self-therapy 44
Sense organs 64
Sensory experiences 34
Sermon on the mount 5
Sex 73
Sexes, affinity between 150
Sexual assaults 75
Sexual desire 21
Sexual instinct 58
Sexual intercourse 153
Shakespeare, William 88
Sheep and goats 10
Shelter, provision of 85
Shunamite 94
Sick, healing of 2, 7, 74, 138–41
Sickness 35
Sikh 101
Sin,
    against the Holy Ghost 101

and free will 115
atoned by Christ 2, 100–1
avoidance of 159
causes suffering 117
communal 98, 119
consequences of 98
expiation of 17, 101
freedom from 108
implies belief in God 116
inducement to 16
knowledge of 111
meaning of 115–6
misuse of the word 116, 122
mystery of 113
problem of 108
propitiation for 10
remission of 84, 96, 97, 100–2
unforgivable 102
Sinful nature 18
Sins, seven deadly 75
Slate, clean 73
Smith, Adam 126
Smoking 22
Social evils 119
Soil,
  fertility of 14
  tillage of 111
Solar panels 130
Soldiers in God's army 36, 43, 46, 53, 55, 60, 64, 67–8, 92, 98
Solomon 118, 135
Son of Man 96
Son, sacrifice of 72
Sorcery 59
Sorrow 33
Soul,
  and mind, one-way traffic between 73
  as a battleground 69, 84
  as armoury 66
  attacked by Satan 74
  attitude of 117
  awareness in 49
  cleansing of 89
  communal 66, 81, 82, 98
  condition of, known only to God 88
  conflict with the intellect 78
  corruption of 16
  creation of 52, 61, 149
  damage to 5, 15, 76
  decisions of 38
  direct communication by 137
  dwells in eternity 136
  growth of 77
  has eternal being 25, 52–3
  implantation of 110
  in heaven 148
  instructions of 38
  is free 65
  is imperfect 13
  its contact with God 21, 53
  its contact with mind 38
  its responsibility for our development 13
  its thaumaturgic powers 136
  linked to God 53
  mode of being of 74
  objectives of 38, 74
  pilgrimage of 12
  pollution of 54
  power of 15
  presence of Christ in 62
  salvation of 20
  task of 12
  the distinguishing feature of humankind 65
Souls,
  are not constrained 72
  are restrained 72
  attain eternal life 103
  can perform miracles 72
  cleansing of 89
  communication between 66
  creation of 52, 114
  creative power of 156
  dwell in eternity 136, 150
  dwell in time and space 136
  have eternal being 25, 52, 65, 72, 90, 114
  immense powers of 136

interaction of 66
latent powers of 136
male and female 149–50
sinfulness of 118
their ability to adapt 150
their entry into eternal life 103
their mission 103
Sound, appreciation of 42
Space and time 28, 52, 114, 136
Species,
   extinction of 31
   imperfect members of 32
   preservation of 15, 30, 32, 42, 47, 122, 154
Speech,
   as used by the soul 65
   freedom of 88
Spirit, as opposed to 'the flesh' 69
Spiritual activity 21
Spiritual communication 65, 137, 141, 143, 147, 152
Spiritual entities 51
Spiritual virus 121
Spirituality, advance in 143
Status, ontological 105
Strategy,
   global 60
   God's 26, 27, 29, 33, 51, 53–5
   of the enemy 66
   our 136
Strife 155
Substance,
   definition of 34f
   mental 46, 89, 90, 105, 141, 149, 156
   of Christ's resurrected body 105
   of consciousness 51
   of matter and mind 34, 46
   of our bodies 90
   of our heavenly bodies 156
   of particles 31
   of physical being 90
   of psychical viruses 89
   of the body 149
   of the Persons of the Trinity 3

of the soul 149
of wave-functions 31
psychical 49
spiritual 149
transformation of 90
Success, assured 72, 125
Suffering 121–2
Suffering,
   bodily 11
   caused by our mistakes 130
   is inevitable 121
   mystery of 113
   transmission of 121
Suicide, universal 130
Sun's rays, heat of 33
Supply and demand, imbalance between 139–40
Supra-eternal being 114, 116, 133
Supra-eternity 56f
Survival,
   instinctual reactions to ensure 80
   mutual, of plants and animals 14
   purposes related to 38
   qualities needed for 14
Survival value 47
Sustaining activity 13, 31, 51, 52, 54, 90, 103
Symbiosis 45
Symphony 77

Tabernacles, Feast of 8
Tabitha 138
Tabula rasa 73
Talents 60
Targets, new 124
Task(s),
   allotted 59
   assigned by God 60
   completion of 64
   confronting us 60, 67
   first 60
   in heaven 147–8, 160
   is formidable 67
   magnitude of 64
   of alien people 64

of an infant 60
of the human race 30
on earth 160
Teachers 61
Technology 60, 86, 99, 109, 113, 130, 131
Teilhard de Chardin, Pierre 48, 50
Telepathy 43, 47, 137, 152
Telephone 86
Television 86, 124, 131
Telos, the,
  consciousness in 49
  control of 43
  defined 32
  distinct from moral sense 154
  dwells in the mind 47
  mind as the agent of 154
  operation of 32, 50
  perversion of 43
  purposes governed by 38
  struggle of 47
Temper,
  contentious 59
  loss of 117
Temple,
  in Jerusalem 7
  moneylenders in 8
Tempo, alteration of 135
Temporal being 3, 13, 28, 32, 50, 114, 133, 146
Temporal life 28, 29, 108, 114, 150, 151, 160
Temporal order 101, 136
Temptation 24, 119
Tennyson, Alfred Lord 55
Territory, acquisition of 130
Tertullian 95
Test 3, 12, 13, 55
Test theory 4, 9, 10, 11, 16, 20, 58, 59, 62, 89
Thalidomide 74
Thankfulness 33
Thanksgiving 89
Thelematic determinations 20
Theologians 28, 61, 143, 157

Thesis and antithesis 84
Third World 128
Thought,
  evil 5
  freedom of 88
  wrongful 117
Time,
  as a point of eternity 151
  beginning of 149
  distinct from eternity 28, 151
  end of 2, 31, 32, 46, 151
  further divine purpose in 151
  is created 151
  is linear 28
  is linked to eternity 150
Time and space,
  annihilation of 151
  contact with, after death 90
  creation of 28, 52, 92, 114, 151
  damaged by Satan 116
  embraced by eternity 40
  laws implanted in 28, 52, 114
  our souls dwell in 136
  world of 38, 72, 90
Timothy 27, 69, 85, 103
Training 62, 67, 89, 98, 106, 108, 130, 141, 148
Transfiguration 95
Trees 47
Tribe 61, 83
Trinity in unity 90
Trinity, the 3, 74
Trust 33
Truth,
  a characteristic of God 27
  appreciation of 36
  concept of 37
  dwells in God 88
  enemies of 83
  in false beliefs 82, 84, 85
  is absolute 88
Truths, theological 78
Turing test 47

Understanding 33, 37–38

Understanding,
   conceptual   38
   positive   96
Unemployment   99, 129, 131
Unhappiness   33
Universe,
   creation of   52, 154
   creatures in   146
   enjoyment of   37
   evolution of   31, 109, 114, 133
   evolves   28
   God's armies in   64
   governance of   102
   has temporal being   31
   immensity of   64, 146
   information about   153
   is created   158
   laws of   13, 15, 29, 30–2, 85, 122, 133, 135, 144, 159
   life in   29
   material, creation of   69
   other beings in   64
   other parts of   92, 125, 146–7
   our allies in   65
   physical   29, 49, 50, 114, 122
   powers extended through   138
   psychical   122
   reason for its creation   38
   structure of   68
Unspiritual nature   18, 59
Utopia   63, 106, 113

Value, all of equal   26
Values,
   materialistic   128
   ultimate   128
Vegetable kingdom   14
Victory,
   a distant goal   67
   assurance of   146, 160
   certainty of   72, 104, 111, 134
Violence   75, 78, 124
Virgin birth   93
Virgin Mary   3
Virtual reality   86, 131

Viruses   14, 29, 74, 89
Viruses,
   psychical   89
   spiritual   121
   substance of   89
Vision, impaired   108
Vocation   61
Volcanoes   14
Vulnerable people   75, 78

War,
   against an invisible enemy   59
   against Satan   *see* under Satan
   aggressive   155
   armoury for   66
   conduct of   53, 59, 62
   defensive   69
   earthly   60
   in heaven   23, 155
   just   5
   nuclear   130
   victory in, certain   72
Warming, global   99
Wars, tribal   83
Wars, worldly   99
Water and the Spirit   11
Wave-function   31
Waves   64
Wealth,
   acquisition of   85
   creation of   127
   increasing   85
   production of   16, 85, 109, 126
Weapon, ultimate defensive   70
Weaponry   67, 88
Weapons,
   and armoury   66–73
   nuclear   100
Well-being, individual   102
Western bloc   128
Western world,
   communal sin of   119
   moral confusion in   139
Why are we here?   57, 59
Wickedness   59

185

Widows 2
Will,
  act of 21
  a faculty of the soul 21
  as driving force 42
  communal 134
  individual 133
  of God *see* Will of God, below
  orientation of 19
  power of 133–4
  subversion of 90
Will of God, the,
  accordance with 44, 45, 145, 148
  alignment with 79, 133
  and control of imagination 37
  and our urge for knowledge 29
  and the creation 30
  and the study of biology 30
  and the telos 43
  attitude of the soul to 117
  attunement with 105
  compliance with, not enforced 148
  evolution in accordance with 137
  frustration of 13
  genetic engineering contrary to 44
  harmonisation of creation with 45
  harmony with, imperilled 53
  is directed to an objective 31
  joy of doing 109
  knowledge of 152
  objective dwelling in 31
  opposition of our will to 54, 134
  opposition of, by Satan 23
  our duty to obey 49
  prayer in accord with 134
  submission to 85, 113, 140, 143
  universal harmony with 45
Wisdom,
  acquisition of 130
  a gift from God 135
  growth in 91, 113, 115
  is fallible 108
  no gene for 135

  prayer for 133–5, 147
Wishful thinking 81
Witchcraft 9
Witch of Endor 5
Womb 110
Words, wrongful 117
World, the,
  beauty of 114
  competition in 14
  contradictions of 14
  co-operation in 14
  darkness of 59
  is good 19
  is imperfect 19
  is not evil 15, 69
  is not opposed to God 15
  knowledge of 73
  laws of 72
  natural 73
  physical 78
  physical and psychical 34
  polluted by humanity 15
  population of 100
  redemption of 53
  reflection of God 15
  rejection of 18
  reveals God's essence 14
  salvation of 97
  sin of 97
  spiritual 69, 154
  structure of 50
  western 84, 98
World war 100
Worlds, spiritual and natural,
  are linked 51
  union of 52
Wrath 122
Writers 61
Writing 66
Wrongdoers, punishment of 80

Zacchaeus 8
Zarephath, widow of 94
Zoroaster 84